Queen Elizabeth II
and the Royal Family in Canada

Golden Jubilee Edition

Queen Elizabeth II
and the Royal Family in Canada

Golden Jubilee Edition

From the Files of The Canadian Press

Edited by PATTI TASKO & RON POLING

Queen Elizabeth (page 1) waves to crowd in
London, Ontario, June 26, 1997. (Frank Gunn)

Queen Elizabeth (page 2) waves as she departs Fort Qu'Appelle,
Saskatchewan, July 29, 1978. (Doug Ball)

Queen Elizabeth (opposite) walks by flag waving
spectators in Saskatchewan. (Dave Buston)

The photographs featured in this book may be acquired for
reproduction by contacting The Canadian Press, 36 King
Street East, Toronto, Ontario M5C 2L9, www.cp.org

The publisher acknowledges the support of the Government of
Canada, Department of Canadian Heritage, Book Publishing
Industry Development Program.

ISBN 1-55082-301-9

Design by Laura Brady <www.bradytypesetting.com>

Printed and bound in Canada by Champlain Graphics,
Pickering, Ontario.

Published by Quarry Press Inc., 195 Allstate Parkway,
Markham, Ontario L3R 4T8.

OUR QUEEN

by Patti Tasko

SHE IS ADMIRED BY MANY and mocked by some, but no matter how you look at it, Queen Elizabeth has made her mark on Canada in the last 50 years. There is hardly a corner of the country where you cannot find evidence of Her Majesty. Her picture appears on our stamps and currency. Her name is on hundreds of roads, hospitals, parks, theatres and schools, even a power station. She is toasted at weddings, and *God Save the Queen*, while not as popular as it once was, is still a tune most Canadians can carry. She gave us our flag and Constitution and helped us celebrate the country's Centennial.

Canada's close relationship with the Queen came early. It was the first Commonwealth country, even beating Britain, to proclaim her as Queen Elizabeth II after the death of King George VI on February 6, 1952.

The relationship may be based largely on nostalgia – many Canadians, who have never known any other monarch, remember her picture, in the white dress, blue sash and crown, hanging in their classrooms at school. But there is also no doubt that she is an accepted icon, even in a multicultural Canada that has not been ruled by Britain for several generations. There has never been a serious move in Canada to get rid of the monarchy, unlike steps taken in other countries such as Australia.

Some of this can be attributed to the magic of television, says David E. Smith, professor of political studies at the University of Saskatchewan and author of *The Invisible Crown*. "One of the characteristics of the Queen's reign is that it has been contemporaneous with the reign of TV," says Smith. "There is a stronger visual presence of the monarchy than there once was – and TV has played a big role in that." This influence started early. Elizabeth's coronation in 1953 was the first one broadcast on TV. "In Canada, TV in some ways has strengthened the respect for the Queen," says Smith. Because of the

Princess Patricia and Major Worthington skating on a small rink in the woods, February 1, 1914. (NAC)

exposure, she has become so familiar to Canadians that the Queen has almost become Canadianized. "Unlike Australians, Canadians don't mind the fact she is British."

Another factor in the acceptance of the monarchy in Canada is the Canadianization of the office of the Governor General, which also coincides with the reign of Elizabeth. Six days before she became Queen, Canada got its first Canadian-born governor general, Vincent Massey. Massey believed that the Crown belonged to Canadians, and as the sovereign's representative his job was to strengthen that bond as well as to promote Canadian unity and identity. The highly regarded Massey and his successor, Georges Vanier, helped keep respect for a made-in-Canada monarchy, says Smith.

The Queen is also personally popular in Canada, and even her detractors might have a hard time arguing she hasn't earned this. She was the first monarch to repeatedly visit. Her Golden Jubilee visit in October 2002 is her 21st official visit.

Her parents, King George VI and Queen Elizabeth, began the tradition of royal tours, as we know them today, in Canada. Although various royal family members had visited or spent time in Canada even before

Confederation, the 1939 coast-to-coast tour by the King and Queen was the first time a sitting monarch had visited. A great deal of Canada's support for the monarchy can be traced to this visit early in George's reign, says Smith. "It made Canada feel special, at an emotional time on the eve of war."

The current Queen picked up this touring tradition early. She first visited Canada as a princess in 1951. Since then, the Queen has been here to celebrate the country's birthday seven times. She opened the St. Lawrence Seaway in 1959, attended Expo 67 and numerous other centenaries. She was at the 1976 Montreal Olympics and the 1978 Commonwealth Games in Edmonton. She has eaten a lot of rubber chicken and shaken countless hands on countless walkabouts in towns from Tofino, British Columbia, to Deer Lake, Newfoundland, and all points in between.

The Queen's family has also carried on the tradition. Of the 80 or so official royal visits that Canada has hosted since 1860, the Queen and members of her immediate family have made 69 of them. Perhaps this happens in every Commonwealth country they visit, but in speeches, Royal Family members often claim a particular fondness for Canada. The Queen's son,

Andrew, took his bride, Sarah Ferguson, on a private canoe trip in the Northwest Territories on their first wedding anniversary. Prince Edward and his wife, Sophie Rhys-Jones, made their first foreign tour as the Earl and Countess of Wessex to Canada's East Coast. Prince Harry, the Queen's grandson, did his first foreign walkabout in Niagara Falls, Ontario, at the age of seven. In the 1970s the Queen Mother stopped travelling to Commonwealth countries – except for Canada, which she continued to visit until 1989.

In the 1950s, royal visits to Canada were long and exhausting. By the end of her six-week 1959 tour, the Queen cancelled some appearances because of illness some attributed to the killer schedule. (Later it was revealed she was also pregnant with Andrew.) The early tours attracted lots of interest in the attractive young Queen and her dashing husband. Every little detail that

The Prince of Wales (King Edward VIII) helps with the roundup at the Bar-U Ranch near High River, Alberta, September 15–16, 1919. (NAC)

could be scratched up was treated as important news. ("Princess Bringing Crinolines," announced a 1951 headline in the *Globe and Mail*.)

"The Queen and Philip, in those days, were the magic that Charles and Diana became in their early relationship," recalls journalist Bruce Levett, who covered the Ontario and Quebec leg of the 1959 tour for The Canadian Press. "I can't recall a single anti-royal incident. Mainly, I remember the small towns with the people cheering and waving flags as the train pulled slowly through."

Most of the tours have been met with enthusiasm, with the notable exception of a 1964 visit to Quebec City to mark the centenary of the talks that led to Confederation. Separatists threatened the Queen's life. "Some of my own people are ready to let her know – and brutally – that she is no longer welcome in French Canada," separatist Marcel Chaput said a few months before the fall trip.

The Queen herself was keen to go. The British government was not in favour, both because of concerns for her safety (John F. Kennedy had been assassinated 11 months earlier) and for what it would do for Britain's reputation if her visit were to be unpopular. But since she was visiting Canada as its Queen, it was up to Prime Minister Lester Pearson to give her advice, and he thought it unnecessary to cancel the trip.

A few hundred protesters greeted her in Quebec City. Municipal police armed with specially issued batons charged the crowd, terrifying and injuring bystanders as well as protesters. "Had it not been for the panicky action by the Quebec municipal police, the visit would have gone off smoothly," scolded an editorial in the *Ottawa Citizen*. Other newspaper columnists suggested that if Quebecers had no reason to hate the Queen before her visit, they did so after officers clubbed innocent people in an attempt to protect her.

Since then, royal family members have returned to Quebec periodically, and the visits have been much more pleasant. The Queen attended Expo 67, although she was surrounded by Mounties. Princess Anne competed at the 1976 Montreal Olympics, and her entire family came out to watch.

King George VI and Queen Elizabeth are received at Parliament Buildings, Ottawa, May 19, 1939, by Prime Minister Mackenzie King. (NAC)

During the Pierre Trudeau years, the obvious presence of Her Majesty in Canadian protocol was diminished. Her likeness fell off many stamps and bank notes, and the letters HM were dropped from government documents. *O Canada* replaced *God Save the Queen*. In 1978 Trudeau introduced a new Constitution that cut the few threads to Britain. Buckingham Palace was not against this, although it did not want Canada to replace the Queen with the Governor General as head of state. The diaries of Paul Martin, Canada's high commissioner in Britain at the time, suggest the Queen's pragmatic handling of the constitutional changes prevented any quarrels from developing between Britain and its former colony.

Four years later, the Queen proclaimed the Constitution at a Parliament Hill ceremony attended by thousands of people. With a smile on her face, she transferred all of her powers to the Governor General. She did keep, however, her title Queen of Canada. Her handling of the constitutional change even won over Trudeau, never a big monarchy supporter whose most famous moment with the Queen before that had been his pirouette behind her back at Buckingham Palace. "The Queen favoured my attempt to reform the

Constitution," he wrote in his memoirs. "I was always impressed not only by the grace she displayed in public at all times, but by the wisdom she showed in private conversation."

In the past 20 years the Queen has continued to visit Canada regularly, although the headlines have been fewer and the crowds smaller. But the visits still mean something to many Canadians, says Geoffrey Lambert, professor of political studies at the University of Manitoba. "Small touches from a famous person go a long way."

The Queen's family has also carried on the visiting tradition first established in 1939. The Queen Mother was a very frequent visitor, with a recurring attraction being the Queen's Plate at Woodbine Racetrack in Toronto, which she first attended with her husband during the 1939 visit when it was, of course, the King's Plate. The oldest consecutive thoroughbred horse race in North America, the Queen's Plate traces its roots

King George VI and Queen Elizabeth on Parliament Hill in October 1939. (NAC)

to 1859, when Queen Victoria agreed to grant a plate worth 50 guineas for the race.

The Queen's sister, Princess Margaret, was also a frequent visitor to Canada. Her first tour, in 1958, was a month long and included dozens of communities in British Columbia, Ontario and the Maritimes. The media liked to portray her as the fun-loving sister, and commented frequently on her miniskirts and daring (by royal standards) lifestyle. Several of her visits were tied to fund-raising efforts for the famous Toronto cancer hospital that bears her name.

Charles has been a visitor to Canada about a dozen times, although he gathered the biggest crowds when his wife Diana, the Princess of Wales, accompanied him in 1983, 1986 and 1991. His children, William and Harry, have also visited twice, and William in particular made headlines when awestruck teen girls tailed him during a 1998 visit to British Columbia. Prince Andrew hasn't just visited Canada – he spent almost a year studying at Lakefield College in eastern Ontario. The Queen's two other children, Anne and Edward, have also done their share of walkabouts on Canadian soil.

During those visits, the Royal Family has only made the most neutral of public comments on Canadian political affairs. It is not known what, if any, role the Queen has played as an adviser to the nine prime ministers who served during her reign. "The Queen is the essence of discreet," says Lambert. A Montreal radio show host did try to catch her out in 1995, on the eve of the Quebec referendum. Posing as Prime Minister Jean Chrétien, Pierre Brassard managed to get the Queen on the phone to discuss the referendum. All she revealed was her hope the separatists would not win. Many callers to the radio station were more struck by her fluent French than her anti-separatist sentiments.

The question now is whether the support for the monarchy in Canada will outlive her. The deaths of the Queen Mother and Princess Margaret in 2002, during the Queen's Golden Jubilee year, seemed to prompt a fondness for the monarchy both in Britain and in Canada. June Jubilee celebrations in Britain were quite energetic and attracted a million people to the streets of London. Charles, in particular, seems to be enjoying a surge in popularity, after several dark years when his marital woes and relationship with Camilla Parker Bowles made him a target of the press.

The feeling in Canada has perhaps been more ambivalent. Since at least 1980, polls have shown that only about half of Canadians support the Queen as their head of state, but getting rid of the monarchy is hardly a burning issue. It would take a constitutional amendment to get rid of the Crown as Canada's head of state, and Canadians have no interest in changing the Constitution – especially for something that isn't going to make a speck of difference in their lives, says John Aimers of the Monarchist League of Canada. Canadian historian Michael Cross of Dalhousie University in Halifax agrees. "How many people lie awake at night worrying about this issue?"

Besides, says Cross, the Royal Family is good entertainment – and this book showcases that. It's a scrapbook of memories for Canadians of the Queen and her family – up close and unfiltered, as written and photographed by the Canadian Press journalists who were there when the Queen came to town.

Canada's national news service has a long tradition, predating the current Queen's reign, of covering royal tours for the country's daily newspapers. Often, the coverage of a royal tour was planned as carefully as a military campaign, with a continual stream of reporters and photographers picking up royals as they moved across the country, by train, boat, automobile and airplane.

From CP's files we have selected the best moments from 50 years of covering the Queen and her family in Canada. CP was there when a princess learned how to square dance in Rideau Hall; when a young Queen first opened Canadian Parliament; when she visited Canada's North for the first time. When her train spent the night on a siding in southern Ontario while local residents chattered with excitement. When she toured an Innu hunting tent in Labrador or a farm in Saskatchewan. When she signed the guestbook in countless city halls in countless communities across this huge country. Those images are all in this book, as are the pictures and voices of hundreds of Canadians, perhaps even someone you know, who crossed paths with royalty in the past 50 years.

THE ROYAL FAMILY OF HER MAJESTY QUEEN ELIZABETH II

Parents: King George VI and Queen Elizabeth (Queen Mother)
King George died 1952. Queen Mother died 2002.

Sister & Spouse: Princess Margaret and the Earl of Snowdon
Divorced 1978. Princess Margaret died 2002.

Husband: The Duke of Edinburgh (Prince Philip)

Children & Spouses: The Prince of Wales (Prince Charles) and Princess of Wales (Princess Diana)
Divorced 1996. Princess Diana died 1997.

The Princess Royal (Princess Anne) and Capt. Mark Phillips
Divorced 1992. Remarried Lt.-Cdr. Timothy Laurence.

The Duke of York (Prince Andrew) and Duchess of York (Sarah Ferguson)
Divorced 1996.

The Earl of Wessex (Prince Edward) and Countess of Wessex (Sophie Rhys-Jones)

Royal Family in Montreal during the 1976 Olympics. Left to right: Prince Philip, Princess Anne, husband Mark Phillips, Prince Edward, Queen Elizabeth II, Prince Andrew and Prince Charles. (Wally Hayes)

Grandchildren: Prince William, son of Prince Charles and Diana
Prince Henry (Harry), son of Prince Charles and Diana

Princess Beatrice, daughter of Prince Andrew and Sarah
Princess Eugenie, daughter of Prince Andrew and Sarah

Peter Phillips, son of Princess Anne and Capt. Mark Philips
Zara Phillips, daughter of Princess Anne and Capt. Mark Philips

———❦———

Line of Succession:
1. Prince of Wales (Prince Charles)
2. Prince William
3. Prince Henry
4. Prince Andrew
5. Princess Beatrice
6. Princess Eugenie
7. Prince Edward
8. Princess Anne

PRINCESS ELIZABETH AND HER DUKE TAKE PART IN HOEDOWN

OTTAWA, OCTOBER 11, 1951 (CP) – Princess Elizabeth went away from the capital today with a lesson in a reviving North American custom. She learned to square dance. So did her big, fun-loving husband, Prince Philip. They got their lesson, of all places, in swank, yet sedate Rideau Hall, the rambling 19th-century home of Governor General Viscount Alexander, as they completed a triumphant two-day official visit to the capital.

Princess Elizabeth and the Duke of Edinburgh square dance at Government House, October 10, 1951. (NAC)

The lesson came at a private dance, the viscount's own private party for the gracious, 25-year-old princess and her sailor husband. There were no reporters or public present, only 70 personal friends of the Viscount and Viscountess Alexander. A lone tour official reported the royal hoedown. The National Film Board took photographs.

From all accounts, the princess and the duke enjoyed the evening. Photographs of the princess show a gay, carefree girl swinging through the brisk strains of the square dance music. She had doffed formal daytime attire to wear a brown-checked blouse and a steel blue flared skirt in the barn-dance style. The duke put on brass-stapled blue jeans for the dance and a white-checked shirt with a red kerchief around his neck.

Those were the costumes the royal couple wore when they slipped away from Rideau Hall about 11 p.m. to head for their 10-car royal train at Ottawa's Union Station. Against the chill night air, the princess wore a mink wrap; the duke a blue overcoat. More than 1,000 persons went to the station to see them

off. They cheered as the royal couple said their good-byes to Viscount and Viscountess Alexander and Prime Minister St. Laurent and Mrs. St. Laurent.

They boarded the train, made one brief platform appearance, then went in for the night. The train pulled out of the capital at 1:06 a.m. EST. As the tired but happy princess tumbled into her berth, she took with her the mellowing memories of two days of thrilling acclaim from tens of thousands who thronged the streets to see her at every stage of the official program.

The princess and her duke did about everything a tourist does in Ottawa. They visited the Parliament Buildings and climbed the soaring heights of the Peace Tower. They browsed through the Public Archives and sampled the French-Canada atmosphere of neighbouring Hull, Quebec. They took a boat trip down the choppy Ottawa River. And they delighted 14,000 Ottawa schoolchildren with an appearance in Lansdowne Park, Exhibition and Sports Centre.

It was the biggest welcome Ottawa has given anyone since the King and Queen came on another royal visit in 1939. An estimated 200,000 persons saw the royal couple.

— George Kitchen

Princess Elizabeth leaves the stage coach at the Calgary Stadium, assisted by Jim Cross, president of the Calgary Stampede Association, October 18, 1951. (NAC)

RCMP restrain enthusiastic crowd during Princess Elizabeth's visit to Winnipeg, October 16, 1951. (NAC)

QUEEN MUM AS
GOVERNOR GENERAL?

Queen Elizabeth strolls in the gardens at Rideau Hall, accompanied by Governor General Vincent Massey and Prince Philip, October 15, 1957. "Duff", a golden retriever, is carrying her handbag. (CP)

OTTAWA, OCTOBER 13, 1957 (CP) – Published suggestions that the Queen Mother might come to Canada as this country's next Governor General appear to have been dampened by Queen Elizabeth.

The Queen seemed surprised Saturday night when, at a press reception in Government House, one reporter asked whether the 57-year-old Queen Mother might succeed Governor General Vincent Massey next spring, an idea which some newspapers in Canada and the United Kingdom have been promoting. "As governor general?" the Queen replied, as though it was the first time she had heard the idea. "My, what a novel idea. Oh, I'm afraid we would miss her too much." She said no more on the subject. Reporters could only speculate on how strongly the Queen and other members of the Royal Family might feel about a prolonged separation from the Queen Mother.

Mr. Massey was appointed early in 1952 for a five-year term, which has been extended one year until next March. Mr. Massey is the first native-born Canadian governor general and the 18th to hold the post since Confederation. All his predecessors were members of the English nobility.

A QUEEN OPENS CANADA'S PARLIAMENT FOR THE FIRST TIME

OTTAWA, OCTOBER 14, 1957 (CP) – With history at its elbow and a nation looking on, Canada's 23rd Parliament was opened today by Elizabeth, Queen of Canada. History was made as a monarch for the first time opened Parliament by reading the speech from the throne. And history was re-enacted in a brilliant ceremony dating back to the days of England's first Queen Elizabeth and earlier.

Prime Minister John Diefenbaker, heading the first Conservative federal government in 22 years, named it the "Queen's Day." Opposition Leader Louis Saint-Laurent, who as prime minister last spring laid plans for this occasion, picked up the phrase. Both said the day would be remembered in Canadian history.

In the red-carpeted Senate chamber, the Queen read the speech from the throne written by her Canadian government, but the speech was more than a recital of government legislation to be introduced in the Parliament's first session.

"I greet you as your Queen," the Queen began, before the assembled Commons and Senate. "Together we constitute the Parliament of Canada … this is for all of us a moment to remember."

The Queen, wearing her coronation gown and a glittering tiara originally owned by Queen Alexandra and Queen Mary, sat on the Senate throne, with Prince Philip at her left. Around her and in the galleries sat dignitaries of the land and brilliantly gowned women. Blazing lights, for television and motion picture cameras, made the chamber uncomfortably warm.

The Commons, back in its own chamber following the throne speech, unanimously adopted a motion expressing loyalty, love, joy and gratitude to the Queen, and sealed the motion with the singing of *God Save the Queen.*

– *by Alan Donnelly*

The Queen and Prince Philip enter the Senate to open Parliament October 14, 1957. Prince Philip wears the uniform of a colonel-in-chief of the Royal Canadian Regiment, the Queen her coronation gown. (CP)

ROYAL BALL TURNS INTO MOB SCENE

MONTREAL, JUNE 26, 1959 (CP) – Thousands of Montrealers danced last night to celebrate the royal visit. About 10,000 danced under the stars in the working-class district of Pointe-St-Charles. And 1,900 formally attired guests of the city of Montreal danced in the great ballroom of the Queen Elizabeth Hotel, creating a terrific crush around the Queen and Prince Philip.

The royal pair gracefully bowed out under the pressure of the huge ballroom crowd, composed of Montreal's most important people. One important person was not there. Frank Hanley, spirited raucous-voiced member of the city council and the provincial legislature, entertained his constituents in highly unregal but festive fashion in Marguerite Bourgeois Park. He said the dance – he called it the "ball of the masses" – was "for working people to honour Her Majesty Queen Elizabeth and Prince Philip." Members of the American Federation of Musicians donated their time to play dance music. Mr. Hanley said he organized it in protest against what he described as the city's "magnificent wastefulness" in paying the shot for its civic ball and banquet. Mr. Hanley said the city should have charged $10 a plate at its banquet and used the money for worthy causes. "I was invited and I would have gone if they did that," he said.

In the hotel, all went well for the early part of the evening. Guests dined and talked gaily during the banquet. Then the orchestra played its first piece, a slow foxtrot. Mayor Sarto Fournier self-consciously took the Queen out onto the dance floor. The mayor had his

Queen Elizabeth exits her car before her visit to Lord Beaverbrook in Fredericton, July 28, 1959. (CP)

troubles. Somehow his hand got tangled slightly in the Queen's silver evening purse, slung over her white-gloved arm. Mayor Fournier was seen signaling behind Her Majesty's back for guests to join in. Most couples only stood and watched.

The first dance ended and the orchestra struck up another tune. The crowd seemed to hesitate, then Prince Philip took the Queen onto the floor. Other couples followed and the crush was on. RCMP officers, who had kept the crowd subdued, withdrew and a mob crowded in toward the royal couple.

Ladies in elaborate evening gowns and men in white ties perched on top of chairs to get a glimpse of the Queen. One lady toppled, sending chinaware clattering to the floor. Chairs were bowled over, waiters and waitresses were jolted and the crowd kept crushing in, squeezing the Queen and the Prince into a small circle.

Mounties formed a wedge to keep the mob back and an appeal was made by a master of ceremonies for the guests to retire. "We couldn't push them as if they were a street mob," one RCMP officer said. "A lot of them were very influential people."

The Queen and Prince finally managed to leave the ballroom. They went to the hotel's royal suite. Queen Elizabeth didn't seem too disturbed through it all. When she withdrew, there was a wide smile on her face. Prince Philip gave a sort of resigned shrug and waved as he disappeared.

"It was the worst example of rudeness and bad manners I've ever seen for a long time," said the wife of an air force officer. "These people are supposed to be the leaders of society in Montreal and they acted like bobby-soxers trying to get a look at Elvis Presley."

Veterans applaud and nurses and spectators crowd in close as Queen Elizabeth visits a veteran's hospital in Victoria, July 17, 1959. (CP)

ROYAL COUPLE CONCLUDES DAY WITH SPARKLING THEATRE VISIT

ABOARD THE ROYAL TRAIN, JULY 2, 1959 (CP) – A day that began in Ottawa in rain and storm ended at Stratford in a night of glittering theatre as the royal tour continued its way across Canada.

After leaving Ottawa around midnight, Queen Elizabeth and Prince Philip went by train to Hamilton Thursday morning, where the Prince broke off for a side trip to London, while the Queen went on through Brantford, Galt, Guelph and Kitchener. They joined again to take in a command performance of *As You Like It* at the Stratford Festival.

The Hamilton visit began at Battlefield House, a two-storey, white rambling farm-house built in 1795. The original home of a family named Gage, it was commandeered by United States forces in 1813. While under arrest, the family, through a youth named

Queen Elizabeth shakes hands with U.S. President Dwight Eisenhower at St. Hubert RCAF base, June 23, 1959, as they prepare to officially open the St. Lawrence Seaway. (Montreal Star)

Billy Green, got a message to the British commander, who attacked in darkness and routed the Americans at the Battle of Stoney Creek. At Hamilton Civic Stadium, the Queen rode standing in a jeep and reviewed the Argyll and Sutherland Highlanders.

More history was in evidence in Brantford, where the Queen signed the Queen Anne Bible, presented in 1712 to "Her Majesty's Church of the Mohawks." All Indian chiefs in attendance except one – E.P. Garlow – wore feathers. "Too darn hot," said the practical Indian.

Thousands turned out in Kitchener – the official police figure was 45,000 – to see the Queen climb the flag-and flower-draped city hall steps. Kitchener gave her a leather-bound picture of her mother and father, taken when

they visited the city in 1939. Running time in Kitchener – 20 minutes.

Back on the train, the Queen retired to her private car but waved to the knots of persons crowding the intersections. Several times the train, speeding up to make up time, slowed to allow the Queen to be seen.

Meanwhile, Prince Philip was in London, where he presented colors to the Royal Canadian Regiment's first and third battalions, just as he had done to the regiment's second battalion in Soest, Germany in 1955.

The royal train parked on a siding outside this festival city, and the prince arrived by car to join his wife. Sharp at 8 p.m., with the sun still hot and the platform lined with men in evening dress and women in formal gowns and furs, the train pulled in. The Queen was radiant in a diamond and pearl tiara and drop diamond earrings. She wore a full-length dress of soft grey, covered with a pale rose design. She carried a white fur stole and wore silver dancing slippers.

From there to the saw-toothed outline of the festival theatre, it was pure pageantry with pipers, drums and bugles. Children hung from trees directly over the royal car and motorcycles forced a way through heavy crowds. Across from the theatre an iron, wind-ing fire escape was crammed from the bottom up for five storeys.

The play pleased the suntanned prince, who leaned forward in his seat several times, smiling and applauding. The audience glittered with uniforms, white and dark formal attire and bare shoulders. However, the Queen was seen to yawn at one stage, and, after a short, formal visit backstage, the royal couple left for the train and a night's sleep parked on a siding between Stratford and London.

Much of the same is in store for them again today – one hour in London, 10 minutes in Chatham, an hour and 45 minutes in Windsor, then aboard the royal yacht *Britannia* and on to Sarnia for a one-hour evening visit.

Thursday's choppy junketing across Ontario by the royal train also took its toll on the press corps. Reporters and photographers were left behind several times and had to race for the train or make their way to the next stop as best they could.   *– by Bruce Levett*

Queen Elizabeth walks around the central theme of the Ottawa memorial to members of the Royal Canadian Air Force at an unveiling ceremony, July 1, 1959. (CP)

QUEEN MOTHER TOURS PIONEER VILLAGE AND ST. LAWRENCE SEAWAY

MORRISBURG, ONTARIO, JUNE 14, 1962 (CP) – The Queen Mother spent an easy and relaxed day along the St. Lawrence Seaway yesterday, wandering through quaint Upper Canada Village and cruising about 25 miles downstream on a navy frigate.

She obviously enjoyed herself in the re-constructed pioneer village, where she visited an old-style tavern and three houses. She chatted with the village's personnel, all decked out in old-fashioned clothing and performing equally old-fashioned tasks. She stopped and chatted with the driver of a team of oxen and laughingly rode in a Farlinger Barouche – and open, horse-drawn carriage.

The Queen Mother, Prime Minister John Diefenbaker, and Governor General Georges Vanier, Ottawa, 1962. (CP)

The Queen Mother spent nearly an hour in the village pointing excitedly at the many items that caught her eye. She had arrived 30 minutes behind schedule after the official cavalcade had slowed down on the 45-minute trip from Ottawa for the benefit of thousands of children who began lining up with their flags three hours before the Queen Mother arrived.

At Winchester nearly every house was flag-bedecked and even the telephone posts were wrapped with red, white and blue bunting. At every intersection along the road, groups gathered to watch the Queen Mother arrive. She was met at the village by Ontario Municipal Affairs Minister Fred Cass and officials of the St. Lawrence Seaway development commission. There were only small crowds to watch her go through the village, and the Queen Mother mingled freely with everyone.

She boarded an RCMP cutter at the Crysler Farm marina not far from the village and was taken about a mile downstream where the navy frigate *Inch Arron* sat with all

flags waiting to entertain the Queen Mother on her four-hour downstream cruise. The cutter was escorted by another RCMP boat and the U.S. Coast Guard.

For her outing the Queen Mother wore a white dress and a white coat lined with rose polka dots. Her petal hat was white with a rose veil. She carried a matching rose-dotted scarf. She rode in a convertible, and during part of her drive around the village, her lady in waiting shielded her from the sun with a white umbrella. The weather was near perfect, with temperatures in the 70s and a pleasant breeze.

After passing through the Iroquois Lock where the frigate was lowered about five feet, the Queen Mother ended her journey at Johnstown, near Prescott, from where she drove back to Ottawa.

The Queen Mother and Colonel K.G. Blackader, colonel of the Black Watch (Royal Highland Regiment) of Canada, attend a regimental mess dinner, June 9, 1962. The Queen Mother was colonel-in-chief of the regiment. (Montreal Star)

The Queen Mother is greeted by Governor General Georges Vanier and Pauline Vanier as she arrives on a brief stopover in Ottawa, March 18, 1966. (CP)

POLICE ROUT SEPARATISTS
DURING QUEEN'S VISIT

QUEBEC, OCTOBER 12, 1964 (CP) – Noisy knots of college-age demonstrators chanting and singing demands for a Quebec independent of the Canadian confederation made the Queen's weekend visit to this normally sedate provincial capital a tense, strident drama.

Thirty-four persons were arrested during the weekend as the Queen rode through streets lined with small numbers of adult citizens and compact groups of the demonstrators whose shouts often dominated the scene. The same separatists, many of them from Montreal, turned up again and again at parade points Saturday and were confronted just as consistently by droves of orange-caped, truncheon-bearing police who looked grim and sometimes showed their determination by charging relentlessly into any groups they considered to be getting out of hand.

As the smiling but slightly nervous Queen drove from point to point of her tour, the separatists chanted, turned their backs and waved their fleur-de-lis flags. At one point, Prince Philip was seen leaning across the Queen to get a better look at the goings-on.

Then came another crisis as the monarch officiated at ceremonies inside the sprawling fortress known as the Citadel. While formalities proceeded within, about 70 youthful separatists sat on a nearby hill chanting but otherwise behaving peaceably. Suddenly, from the bottom of a long slope appeared splotches of orange that denoted the approach of the helmeted municipal lawmen. The demonstrators chanted some more, then headed off toward the city, prodded from behind.

All disappeared into the central city, but Mark Schlieffer, a gaunt-looking bearded New Yorker, was struck by four baton-bearing police and placed roughly under arrest. Reporters who saw the incident protested to police.

The separatists, meantime, were circulating through the city, awaiting another chance to vent their grievances within view of the Queen. A big opportunity came as she and Prince Philip, riding in a closed, bulletproof car, were taken under heavy guard to the Chateau Frontenac Hotel for a Saturday night state dinner. A group of separatists yelled their slogans in college-cheer fashion, watched by scores of city officers – still grim-looking, but apparent less prone to violent measures – together with lines of RCMP, Quebec provincial police and puzzled-looking members of the army and air force.

The Queen and Philip waved a smiling response to the shouts, and the separatists, surrounded by dozens of cameramen, headed down narrow, troop-lined St-Louis Street in the wake of the royal passage toward the Chateau. Near the massive, turreted hotel, police charged into the column of demonstrators, putting their leaders to flight and leaving the column a headless shambles.

More chanting greeted the Queen after she emerged from the dinner, and further incidents occurred along downtown St-Jean Street as some of the youths paraded in roundabout fashion to the city hall. There they were put to flight and demonstrations fizzled out under a heavy cloak of police vigilance.

Police struggle with a demonstrator taken into custody October 10, 1964, just outside the legislative buildings in Quebec City as Queen Elizabeth arrives for a state visit. (CP)

HI, QUEEN,
HI, DUKE

OTTAWA, JULY 1, 1967 (CP) – A sandy-haired youngster in blue jeans upstaged royalty at Canada's birthday-cake party today by scampering through security guards to share a platform briefly with the Queen and Prince Philip.

A crowd of more than 50,000 was on Parliament Hill as the six-year-old boy got within speaking range of the royal couple. "Hi Queen," he said, waving a small Maple Leaf flag for a broadly smiling Elizabeth. As State Secretary Judy LaMarsh, organizer of the party, smiled and Mounties tore their hair, the boy sidled over to Philip. "Hi, Duke," he said.

Flustered officials finally shoed the youngster backstage where, resplendent in his red, white and blue T-shirt, he was kept quiet by Toronto trumpeter Bobby Gimby while royalty took over the show.

"Wasn't that little kid great?" Miss LaMarsh remarked afterwards.

Prince Philip nibbled the icing but got no deeper into the cake marking Canada's centennial celebration of Confederation. The giant plywood cake, shimmering with genuine white icing, towered over the Queen as she sliced into a small fruit cake inserted into the five-foot-high bottom tier. The royal slice was the signal for the crowd to burst into cheers as hundreds of balloons were set loose to drift across the cloudless sky.

The day was designed by Miss LaMarsh for children, from her specially-requested "mushy" icing on 40,000 birthday cupcakes to special seats on the dais for about 300 handicapped youngsters.

The emphasis on children extended to the gifts presented to the royal couple for their

own youngsters. Denise Larrean, 16, and Steven Kennedy, 13, presented books, records of the *Ca-na-da* song and a wooden snowmobile to the Queen. The two young people represented the handicapped children of Ottawa.

The Queen wore a chalk-white sleeveless A-line dress in ribbed cotton and a hat made out of little flowers with their stems forming the crown. She had planned to wear a matching white coat, but the brilliant 81-degree sunshine made her decide to leave the coat at Government House.

OTTAWA, JULY 4, 1967 (CP) – Thousands saw six-year-old John Brack wander up onto a platform here Saturday to meet the Queen, but his parents weren't among the onlookers. Mr. and Mrs. David Brack didn't even believe John when he told them later that he had shaken hands with Queen Elizabeth. Mr. Brack said the truth of the story only dawned when the family watched a television newscast that night.

They lost John for a few minutes Saturday in the huge crowd at a Centennial birthday party on Parliament Hill. Dignitaries on the platform watched in fascination as John sauntered between lines of Mounties to the royal couple and said:

"Hello Queen, hello Duke."

"Hello sonny," Prince Philip replied.

The Bracks, who were looking for John in the huge crowd, missed the incident. They found him a few minutes later at the Centennial flame, a meeting place they had agreed on beforehand in case of separation.

"He's been brought up to know the Queen as Andy's mother," said Mr. Brack, referring to Prince Andrew, who is the same age as John.

Queen Elizabeth looks down from atop the mini-rail at Expo 67 during her tour of the site with Prime Minister Lester B. Pearson, July 3, 1967. (CP)

COMPUTER WELCOMES
PRINCESS MARGARET

A beaver (right foreground) peeks out of his box at a July 14, 1970 ceremony at Lower Fort Garry, Manitoba. The Hudson's Bay Company observed an old tradition, in which two beavers were presented to Queen Elizabeth by Viscount Armory, governor of the company. Beavers are part of payment traditionally made by the company when a ruling monarch visits the Canadian West. (CP)

TORONTO, OCTOBER 7, 1967 (CP) – A talkative computer startled Princess Margaret yesterday when she visited a cancer hospital named in her honour. She and her husband, Lord Snowdon, were inspecting computer equipment when a message abruptly flashed on a screen.

"We welcome your royal highness to the Princess Margaret Hospital."

"Why thank you," said the startled princess.

The smiling princess, wearing a soft white double-breasted near mini-coat, left a lot of bubbling enthusiasm in her wake as she toured the hospital, frequently leaving her husband and photographers behind.

She and Lord Snowdon arrived here Thursday on a private visit to Canada. They attended a ball last night, the primary reason for their Toronto visit, to raise money for the hospital. They leave here today for a five-day visit to Expo 67.

During her hospital tour, she and her husband posed for Ian Wilson, 14, a third-floor patient who asked if he could take their pictures. Mary Beth Allen, a 10-year-old patient, wanted to meet Princess Margaret so she marched up to her and began to talk. She described her parents' recent visit to England, and wrung every heart in the room when she said: "And I can tell you something else, too. My mommy and I never thought I'd be able to go to school."

At a luncheon at the hospital lodge, the princess was presented with a mink stole and Lord Snowdon with a copy of Roloff Beny's collection of photographs of Canada. Indian handmade toys were given them for their children.

GRUELLING SCHEDULE FOR ROYAL FAMILY'S TOUR OF ARCTIC

TUKTOYAKTUK, JULY 7, 1970 (CP) – The Royal Family crossed the Northwest Passage on Monday in a gruelling second day of their Arctic tour. The Queen and Princess Anne travelled about 1,800 miles by air, visiting an Inuit village at Resolute and flying on to Inuvik before the last event of the day – a flight to Tuktoyaktuk to see the midnight sun. As it turned out the sun was hidden behind clouds over the northern sea. Prince Philip and Prince Charles flew about 2,400 miles, also taking the Frobisher-Resolute-Inuvik route, but making a 575-mile detour by air force Hercules to see Panarctic Oil Ltd. Exploration sites on Melville Island.

The Royal Family travelled from Inuvik to Tuk, as the natives call it, in two Twin Otters – one owned by the RCMP and the other by

Queen Elizabeth and Prince Philip at Government House, June 30, 1970. (Chuck Mitchell)

Imperial Oil Ltd. The temperature was 41 Fahrenheit, a stiff breeze was blowing off the Beaufort Sea, and it was raining as the Royal Family rode through the bumpy streets of this hamlet of 600. About 500 of the year-round residents are Inuit.

Chained sled dogs snarled, barked, wagged their tails and put on a great show for the visitors. Children streamed though the streets behind the two station wagons, which carried the royal visitors, and six trucks in the cavalcade. The visitors wore the parkas given them Sunday at Frobisher Bay, where they began their tour.

They visited a pingo – a huge ice boil in which the Inuit here are carving a curling rink. The Inuit placed a tundra-coloured rug on the icy floor. But the royalty was mostly

impressed by the magnificent crystallized ice of the ceiling. They also visited a fur shop and a sod hut of the type Inuit lived in before modern houses were built here.

Tuk is a trans-shipment point at the delta of the Mackenzie River. A Distant Early Warning radar base is located on a hill just outside of town. The town is connected to the outside world by a single telephone.

Most of the village residents filled the school gymnasium to see the first royal visitors to the Arctic.

"That's Prince Charles right there," a mother told her child. "Prince Charles, that's Princess Anne's brother. And that's his mother, the Queen. And that other man with hardly any hair, Prince Philip, that's her dad."

An elderly Inuit woman in a long fur coat was led away by Territorial Commissioner Stu Hodgson after she went up to the royal visitors and leaned over and touched Prince Charles with a toothless grin. The prince broke up.

Prince Charles dances with Jocelyn Rouleau, 21, niece of Prime Minister Pierre Trudeau, at a dinner-dance in Government House in Ottawa, July 4, 1970. (Rod MacIvor)

"Gee, that's nice," another elderly woman said. "I never thought I'd live to see the Queen in Tuk."

After a drum dance by the expert hamlet troupe, that royal visitors returned to Inuvik and got to sleep at the Anglican mission there at 2 a.m. MST. Their day had started in Frobisher at 7 a.m. EDT.

– *by Gerard McNeil*

Norah Michener, wife of the Governor-General Roland Michener (centre), curtsies to Prince Charles as the Prince and Princess Anne leave Winnipeg, July 16, 1970 for Washington. (Peter Bregg)

Princess Anne, Queen Elizabeth and Prince Philip (next page) sail to Victoria, May 3, 1971, accompanied out of Vancouver harbour by numerous small craft. (Bill Croke)

QUEEN'S SPEECHES INDICATE STRONGER POLITICAL POSTURE

CALGARY, JULY 7, 1973 (CP) – Queen Elizabeth arrived back in London Friday after mapping a more aggressive, political role for the modern monarchy in Canada. Through-out travels in Ontario, Prince Edward Island, Saskatchewan and Alberta during the last 11 days, the 47-year-old monarch stressed the unifying role of the Crown.

"It is as the Queen of Canada that I am here," she told a Toronto audience on the second day of the 3,400-mile trip. "Queen of Canada and all Canadians, not just one or two ancestral strains."

On the final day here, during a chaotic meeting with Alberta Indian chiefs, she pledged governmental support for Indian efforts aimed at enforcing treaties signed by her great-great-grandmother Queen Victoria, nearly a century ago. "You may be assured that my government of Canada recognizes the importance of full compliance with the spirit and terms of your treaties," she told the 42 chiefs.

Under the treaties, the Crown, through the Canadian government, promised to provide health care, education services and opportunities for economic development in exchange for shared use of the county's land. Indian spokesmen said later they would be able to turn to the Crown for redress if they are unsatisfied by future treatment from Ottawa. Her stand was apparently accepted happily by the government and the estimated 1.2 million people who glimpsed her during her visit.

The tour itself ranged from the reserved to the rambunctious. The six-day hop

Queen Elizabeth enjoys a performance of Indian dancing at Mount McKay, in Thunder Bay, July 3, 1973. Sitting with the Queen was Chief Leonard Pelletier of the Fort William Indian Band. (CP)

Harold Cardinal, president of the Alberta Indian Association, watches as Queen Elizabeth emerges from a teepee at an Indian village in Calgary, July 5, 1973. (CP)

Queen Elizabeth and Prince Philip ride in an open carriage on the way to the Ontario legislature at Queen's Park to hear Premier William Davis deliver an address, June 26, 1973. (CP)

through Ontario most satisfied the royal couple's expressed desire to "meet the people." More than a million caught a glimpse of them during that stretch, which included stops at Cobourg and Kingston on the north shore of Lake Ontario and others at London, Cambridge, Kitchener, St. Catharines and Niagara-on-the-Lake. They watched one of the tour's two plays at the Shaw Festival in Niagara-on-the-Lake following a colourful Fort George ceremony earlier in the day.

Pressing throngs in Ontario gave way to reflective gatherings celebrating the 100th birthday of Prince Edward Island. Dazzling pageantry on the RCMP training grounds in Regina, where the centennial of the Mounties was marked, contrasted with rough-and-ready cowboy bedlam at the opening of the Calgary Stampede.

But the Queen appeared relaxed and appreciative through it all. Stately moments during the tour often gave way to ones of outright hilarity. In Thunder Bay, during a two-hour stop, the royal couple had one of the funniest moments.

Mayor Walter Assef, a former vaudeville comedian, threw off the normally rigid ways to thank Prince Philip for bringing his "gracious wife" to town. The mayor, doing a little dance on the city hall steps, had the royal couple laughing uproariously.

One of the only potentially uncomfortable moments came during the Regina stop, when Chief David Ahenakew of Prince Albert injected a plea for Indian rights. The chief criticized the government for the "yoke of dependence" it had imposed on Indians and urged the Queen to notice the wrong-doings of her servants in government. But the incident passed easily, the Queen nodding and murmuring "thank you" after Ahenakew made his plea. The following day, she answered him in her Calgary address.

One of those most pleased with the visit was Prime Minister Pierre Trudeau, who has given the impression of playing down the monarchy in the past. He fell into line with the Crown during the tour, reflecting fully the Queen's words that it be used as a unifying tool for all Canadians.
                                                    – by Doug Small

Queen Elizabeth gets a mini-train tour of Ontario Place following her arrival in Toronto, June 25, 1973. Prince Philip rides in the next compartment of the tour train. (CP)

Queen Elizabeth is presented with flowers by Trina Pelletier, 7, daughter of Chief Leonard Pelletier, during her visit to Mount McKay in Thunder Bay, July 3, 1973. Trina was the Easter Seal Tammy for 1973. (CP)

E.P. Taylor, president of the Ontario Jockey Club, escorts Queen Elizabeth past crowds at Woodbine Racetrack in Toronto, June 30, 1973. (CP)

The Queen Mother (next page) waves and smiles as she says goodbye after spending the day in Montreal, June 27, 1974. (Doug Ball)

The Queen accepts a gift of one of the RCMP's horses during a visit to the RCMP training depot at Regina, July 4, 1973, where she and Prince Philip took part in ceremonies marking the RCMP's Centennial. (CP)

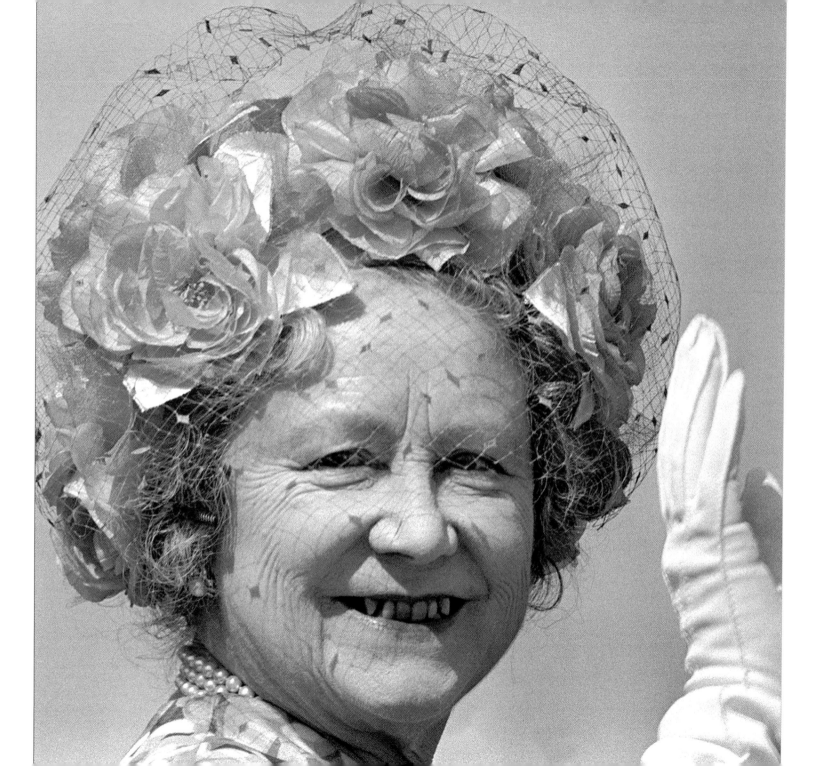

PRINCE CHARLES WRITES SONG FOR VILLAGE DINNER

Garbed in wolverine-trimmed parka and rabbit fur hat, Prince Charles laughs while watching an ice house building competition in Frobisher Bay, April 25, 1975, during festivities to mark the local Toonik Tyme Festival and Charles' visit. (Doug Ball)

YELLOWKNIFE, APRIL 28, 1975 (CP) – Prince Charles landed here Sunday night on the final lap of his whirlwind tour of the North, fresh from two quick afternoon visits in the High Arctic.

After a relaxed and humorous evening in Resolute Bay on Saturday, Prince Charles visited the budding gas fields on King Christian Island and stopped off at Pelly Mission before flying south to the territorial capital for the last two days of his visit.

The aircraft carrying the 26-year-old heir to the throne tried to land at Beechey Island, site of a memorial to the North Pole expedition of ill-fated Sir John Franklin, lost more than 100 years ago. But chancy weather that has plagued the tour since it started from Ottawa on Wednesday closed the island airport down and the Prince was diverted to Pelly Mission on the mainland, where he chatted briefly with the inhabitants. The tour then turned back from the High Arctic and came here for a two-day visit in and around Yellowknife.

The flight south came after an unusual and entertaining evening Saturday in Resolute Bay, during which the prince and his press contingent combined to provide the entertainment at a dinner given by the village council. After the dinner the prince, who has done his best to be relaxed and informal throughout the tour, let his hair down all the way.

After the press group had sung three songs written as they flew through the grey northern skies, Charles rose, took a slip of paper from his pocket, and said: "We can't let this go without a reply."

Then, to the tune of an old British hymn, he and his personal staff sang their own song, one line of which went: "Oh where, may I ask, is the monarchy going; when princes and pressmen are on the same Boeing."

The song ended with a verse describing the shambles made of the carefully created tour plan by the weather, then Charles, beaming his broadest, sat back down to the ringing cheers and applause of the full assembly.

Prior to all this, the prince, a qualified Royal Navy diver, had joined Dr. Joseph MacInnis in a dive beneath the thick blue ice of Resolute Bay. Dropping through a hole cut in the ice, Charles, MacInnis and Rick Mason explored fresh-water icicles dangling from the bottom of the ice. They then plunged to 30 feet in the frigid waters to inspect what MacInnis called a black hole, a depression in the seabed filled with oil-like substances. MacInnis blamed them on oil spills.

Prince Charles, his miner's hat aglow, is somewhat muddied as he leaves the Con gold mine in Yellowknife, April 28, 1975 after a trip 3,100 feet underground. (Doug Ball)

Charles dances with Gaby Leger, wife of Governor General Jules Leger, at a Government House ball, April 23, 1975. (Doug Ball)

Charles gets his chance to fine-tune his mushing skills as he leads a team of dogs in Colville Lake, April 26, 1975. (Doug Ball)

QUEEN WATCHES ANNE'S ALMOST FLAWLESS EQUESTRIAN PERFORMANCE AT OLYMPICS

MONTREAL, JULY 26, 1976 – Queen Elizabeth left for London by plane early today, ending a 20-day tour of Canada and the United States that included a week of enthusiastic welcomes from Quebecers – not noted for their fondness for the monarchy. While most members of the warm crowds that showed up to greet her were English-speaking, there were no signs of any deep-seated resentment of the Queen's visit, which was highlighted by her opening of the Olympic Games. Although there had been criticism about the decision to invite the Queen to open the Games, the few protests organized while she was here appeared to have little support.

Saturday, she was guest of honour at a reception at the downtown Queen Elizabeth Hotel. Prime Minister Pierre Trudeau welcomed the Royal Family to Canada and

Queen Elizabeth flashes a smile for Montreal Mayor Jean Drapeau at a reception at Montreal city hall, July 17, 1976. (Wally Hayes)

expressed his loyalty to the Queen and his pleasure at having the entire family in Canada for the first time. For her part, the Queen called Montreal "a living act of faith in the ideal which Canada represents to the world."

About 2,000 people attended the reception, followed by a dinner for 200 guests. They represented all levels of government, with several federal cabinet ministers and Supreme Court judges present. The prime minister presented the Queen with a gold-plated miniature of an Olympic shield sculpture by Dr. Tait McKenzie, Canadian surgeon, sculptor, athlete and soldier. It depicts the Olympic spirit and features the Olympic slogan – stronger, higher, swifter.

The Queen had a full day Sunday, highlighted by watching Anne ride well on the final day of the Olympic equestrian event at

Prince Philip gives Princess Anne a few words of advice while Queen Elizabeth, Prince Charles and Prince Andrew listen in prior to her starting in the Olymptic cross-country three day equestrian event at Bromont, Quebec, July 24, 1976. (Chuck Mitchell)

Princess Anne (previous page) riding in the three day equestrian event in Bromont, Quebec, July 22, 1976. (Chuck Mitchell)

Margaret Trudeau, wife of Prime Minister Pierre Trudeau, holds an animated conversation with Prince Charles at a posh reception attended by Queen Elizabeth and the Canadian prime minister. (CP)

Bromont, 50 miles east of here. Although there was some cloud, it was a good day for the equestrian competitions. This contrasted with the rain showers that marred Saturday's cross-country event, which saw Princess Anne fall from her horse and suffer a mild concussion. At a news conference Sunday with the rest of the British equestrian team, Princess Anne said: "I'm feeling all right, but I'm still a bit stiff."

The Queen spent more than three hours at the equestrian event and watched Princess Anne give an almost flawless performance in her jumping before the appreciative crowd.

Earlier in the day, the Queen attended a church service at the 150-year-old St. John's Anglican Church in Bromont with Prince Andrew, Prince Charles and Prince Edward. Later, she and her sons visited the Bromont Olympic village and saw the apartment where Princess Anne has been staying. Before going their separate ways, the whole family posed for photographers on a lawn at the private home where Prince Philip has been staying.

The Queen, Prince Andrew and Prince Edward flew home together on Sunday evening. Prince Charles flew home separately. Prince Philip, Princess Anne and her husband Capt. Mark Phillips are to remain for the rest of the Olympics. Anne, a member of the British Olympic equestrian team, is expected to march in the Olympic Games closing ceremony next Sunday.

Queen Elizabeth watches events during the Montreal Olympics, July 1976. (Wally Hayes)

25-FOOT GAP BETWEEN QUEEN
AND SEPARATIST PREMIER

Queen Elizabeth and Prince Philip (previous page) wave to waiting crowds as the royal couple ride in an open carriage during Silver Jubilee celebrations, escorted by Royal Canadian Mounted Police to Parliament Hill, October 18, 1977. (Andy Clark)

The Queen is greeted by a salute of oars at Ottawa's Dow's Lake where she went to watch the Silver Jubilee regatta, October 15, 1977. (Ron Poling)

OTTAWA, OCTOBER 17, 1977 (CP) – Premier René Levesque had little time yesterday to talk to the Queen about Quebec separation – as he had said he might do – because a luncheon seating plan placed him about 25 feet from the monarch.

Mr. Levesque had said under questioning at a press conference earlier this month that he would make his views on separation clear to the Queen if the subject came up at the luncheon given for the Queen, Prince Philip and provincial premiers and their wives at Prime Minister Pierre Trudeau's Harrington Lake residence. Later, he called the remark a half-joke.

When he sat down for the four-course meal complete with champagne, the Queen sat at one end of the table, with Mr. Trudeau and Ontario Premier William Davis on either side. Mr. Levesque was beside Prince Philip at the other end.

"It's the prime minister's seating plan," a Trudeau aide said.

Mr. Levesque had a brief chance to talk with the Queen when the premiers and their wives were introduced soon after she arrived 30 minutes late from Wakefield, Quebec. Later, the Queen approached Mr. Levesque, who was standing with his back to a roaring fireplace, and chatted with him while the chain-smoking premier held a burning cigarette behind his back.

She then turned and engaged in animated conversation with premiers Alex Campbell of Prince Edward Island, Gerald Regan of Nova Scotia and Allan Blakeney of Saskatchewan

Queen Elizabeth talks with Cree singer Buffy Saint-Marie (in native dress) and members of her band after their royal concert at Ottawa's National Arts Centre, October 16, 1977. (CP)

while Mr. Levesque continued to take puffs from the cigarette, exhaling the smoke through his nostrils and placing the butt behind his back each time. Mr. Levesque left immediately after the luncheon and was not available for questioning on what he and the Queen talked about.

"We're late but we enjoyed it," the Queen said to Mr. Trudeau of the trip to Wakefield as he greeted her on the veranda steps of the cottage. She was bundled up warmly against the chilly air in a maize-colour coat with fitted front and full back with strapped sleeves and a matching velvet tam-o-shanter with brown silk tassel. She also wore light-coloured gloves. When she removed her coat at the cottage, she revealed a pale maize-coloured dress with brown coin spots, a seamed panel front and three-quarter sleeves.

The arrival earlier of Mr. Levesque in a black limousine flying Quebec's fleur-de-lis flag caused a stir among reporters who asked him if he had anything to say before his meeting with the Queen. "I'm hungry," he said, as he brushed by, not noticing that Mr. Trudeau was standing to greet him at the opposite side of the veranda.

"You could at least say hello," Mr. Trudeau called over the premier's shoulder just as he was about to go in the door.

"Oh, hello," said a surprised Mr. Levesque, turning with his hand outstretched. The two shook hands, smiled and entered the cottage.

On seeing the Quebec flag on the car, Mr. Trudeau quipped to reporters, "What flag is that?"

Also attending was Manitoba's premier-elect Sterling Lyon and his wife. Progressive Conservatives won a majority in last week's Manitoba election.

'Who's this?" Mr. Trudeau joked as Mr. Lyon was driven up to the front of the cottage.

"You must be a new guy," he said, shaking Mr. Lyon's hand.

The guests sipped sherry and cocktails before lunch. The Queen, as is her custom, took a mineral water with a slice of lemon while Prince Philip had a bloody Mary.

Lunch consisted of trout stuffed with salmon, James Bay blue goose, an endive salad, Oka cheese and sugar pie tarts. It was washed down with Quebec mineral water and Dom Perignon champagne.

Mr. Trudeau's wife, Margaret, was not present at the luncheon, but a large colour photo of her rested on a table and leaned against one wall in the room.

Prince Andrew, wearing his Lakefield school T-shirt, tries his skis while practising with the Lakefield College ski team at Cedar Mountain, near Lakefield, Ontario, January 21, 1977. (Blaise Edwards)

UNITY MAIN THEME OF QUEEN'S SILVER JUBILEE SPEECHES

Queen Elizabeth and Prince Philip seated in their thrones in the Senate Chambers, wait for members of Parliament to be called to hear the Queen read the throne speech, October 18, 1977, officially opening the session of Parliament. (CP)

OTTAWA, OCTOBER 19, 1977 (CP) – Four tiara and black-tie dinners behind them, Queen Elizabeth and Prince Philip leave Canada today for the Caribbean to continue their Silver Jubilee tour of the Commonwealth, an appeal for Canadian unity the message of their six-day visit here. The Silver Jubilee visit was the 10th to Canada of the Queen's 25-year reign and the first since a separatist government was elected in Quebec last November.

The Queen emphasized the benefits of Confederation in an address telecast to the nation Sunday night, a message that was reiterated Tuesday when she opened a new session of Parliament. In the speech from the throne, read to assembled members of Parliament, senators and high judges, the Queen emphasized the success of Canadians in establishing "a vigorous democracy well suited to a proud and free people. A generation of Canadians has been born, and grown to maturity during my reign. I know you will understand when I say that I have a special interest in these young men and women, contemporaries of our own children. They are people made strong by the achievements of their parents and grandparents, but not imprisoned by the prejudices of the past. In their sensitivity towards other people, in their sense of justice, in their generosity and good will, lie not only lessons for us all, but also the best and surest hope for unity and understanding among Canadians everywhere."

The speech, read by the Queen but written by the Trudeau government, emphasized the

economic strength and opportunity Canada offers, but also admitted the difficulty the government has had in dealing with unemployment and inflation.

In Sunday night's speech, the Queen described Canada as an illustration that "man's finer instincts can prevail." The country offered citizens opportunity, freedom, peace and security. "You live in peace, you enjoy, a standard of living higher than 92 per cent of the world's population and you live in a democracy, with real civil liberties and human rights," she said in the speech televised live from Government House.

The steady rain that dogged the visit gave way to leaden skies Tuesday that allowed the royal couple to ride from Government House to Parliament in an open carriage pulled by four black horses. Members of the RCMP musical ride provided the escort for the 20-minute trip through crowd-thronged streets.

The Queen, wearing a tiara and fur-lined silver gown and sitting in buffalo robes in the landau, and Prince Philip, dressed in his field marshal's uniform, waved and smiled at lines of spectators along the 2.2-mile route. A crowd estimated by RCMP at 10,000 was on Parliament Hill for the arrival of the landau, and 41 scarlet-clad, lance-bearing Mounties on black horses moving at a brisk and bobbing trot. Soldiers of the Royal 22nd Regiment, wearing scarlet and bearskin hats, stood at attention as the carriage arrived. A 21-gun salute boomed out and 15 military jets roared over the Peace Tower in a military salute.

In the Senate, the Queen donned glasses to read the speech from the throne. Officials said it was the first time she has done so on such an occasion.

A group of women crowd around a window at Old Fort York in Toronto to get a glimpse of the Queen Mother taking tea with dignitaries, July 1, 1979. (Andy Clark)

QUEEN MUM, DAUGHTER AND GRANDDAUGHTER CROSS PATHS IN TORONTO

TORONTO, JULY 7, 1981 (CP) – The province of Ontario, revelling in the second visit of the Queen Mother in three years, put on a royal bash yesterday and invited her to return. And as the dinner party got underway, Princess Margaret flew into Toronto for a week-long Ontario visit. Her daughter, Lady Sarah Armstrong-Jones, 17, accompanied her.

The three met briefly, after the formal dinner thrown in the Queen Mother's honour at the Royal York Hotel. Premier William Davis, straying from his prepared text at the dinner, told Her Majesty: "We welcome you to your home-away-from-home and hope you feel comfortable in returning to our province ... whenever it can be arranged."

The Queen Mother accepts a bouquet of flowers from seven-year-old Jacqueline Elizabeth Borosa, in Toronto, July 2, 1981, during a seven-day visit to Canada. (Gary Hershorn)

Three generations of royalty assemble at the Royal York Hotel in Toronto, July 6, 1981, as left to right, Lady Sarah Armstrong-Jones, the Queen Mother and Princess Margaret met before a dinner given by Ontario Premier Bill Davis. (Bill Becker)

The Queen Mother listens to ceremonies during her visit to Niagara-on-the-Lake, July 6, 1981. (Bill Becker)

The Queen Mother said she hoped to return to Canada soon. "Alas, I shall set out for England (today), but I will be heartened by the many kindnesses I have received," she told the gathering of 1,100 invited guests. "I hope sincerely it won't be too long before I'm with you all again."

Princess Margaret, 50, stepped from the Canadian Forces Cosmopolitan twin-propelled aircraft to a 21-gun salute and a royal salute from an honor guard of the Lorne Scots Regiment. Today, the princess is to visit the Variety Village sport and fitness centre for the disabled. She is also scheduled to attend a ballet performance where Irish Republican Army sympathizers have said they will protest British policies in Northern Ireland. Also on the itinerary for her Ontario visit, which ends next Monday, are trips to Ontario Place in Toronto and a mine in Timmins.

Princess Margaret tours the Kidd Creek Mine in Timmins, decked out in all of the necessary accessories including hard hat and flashlight, July 9, 1981. (Bill Becker)

CONSTITUTION
COMES HOME

OTTAWA, APRIL 17, 1982 (CP) – The Constitution is "truly Canadian at last," the Queen said today as she declared again her "undoubted confidence in the future of this wonderful country."

One hundred and fifteen years after Confederation, Canada is at last truly independent. The updated Constitution, wiping out the last vestige of British control over its former colony, became law today as Queen Elizabeth signed a royal proclamation amid trumpeted salutes, booming cannons and cheering crowds on Parliament Hill. With a historic stroke of a fountain pen, the Queen signed into effect a Constitution including a Charter of Rights and the power to change the supreme law of the land without going cap in hand to Britain for approval.

Queen Elizabeth (previous page) attends a dinner given in her honour by New Brunswick Premier Richard Hatfield, in Moncton, September 25, 1984. (Julien LeBourdais)

The only sombre note came as the Quebec government, lone opponent of the federal-provincial accord that led to patriation, declared war on the new Constitution in nearby Hull, Quebec, and organized a protest march in Montreal for later today. The absence of Quebec is regrettable, the Queen said, switching to French in her speech before thousands moments after the historic signing

A huge portrait of Queen Elizabeth and the Duke of Edinburgh is put up in downtown Ottawa, April 15, 1982, as the Queen arrives to proclaim the return of Canada's Constitution. (Andy Clark)

Portrait photographer Yousuf Karsh is shown at his Ottawa studio with an exposure he created of Queen Elizabeth. (Ron Poling)

ceremony. But it is still "right to associate the people of Quebec with this celebration because, without them, Canada would not be what it is today," she said.

Prime Minister Pierre Trudeau also regretted the Parti Québécois government's decision to reject his cherished new Constitution but said "nothing essential to the originality of Quebec has been sacrificed. Moreover, the process of constitutional reform has not come to an end. The two orders of government have made a solemn pledge to define more precisely the rights of native peoples. At the same time, they must work together to strengthen the Charter of Rights, including language rights in the various provinces."

But even these reminders of the split between Canada's two solitudes cast no apparent pall over the televised celebration in the national capital. As the royal standard flew above the Parliament Buildings, the Queen strode from her throne on a raised red-carpeted dais to a nearby mahogany table where she signed the ornate document. Trumpeters sounded a royal fanfare while a beaming trio – Trudeau, Justice Minister Jean Chrétien and Registrar General André Ouellet – added their signatures. The proclamation was then read by Huguette Labelle, undersecretary of state.

Among the 1,500 guests seated in bleachers on either side of the dais were MPs, senators and all premiers, except René Levesque of Quebec, lone holdout on the November 5, 1981 federal-provincial deal that led to patriation.

The Queen, sparkling in white silk, rubies and diamonds, capped her busy day of constitution ceremony at a glittering state dinner tonight with politicians, top bureaucrats and others who helped in the patriation process. It was a crowning social event for more than 100 dignitaries, many of whom were closely involved for months, even years, in the negotiations and related activities that came to a head this morning with official proclamation of the Canada Act.

The guests, most in husband-wife couples, were dressed to the hilt, and the Queen examined virtually every one of them from head to toe as they passed through a pre-dinner reception line where she was accompanied by Prince Philip, Governor General Ed Schreyer and his wife, Lily.

Queen Elizabeth signs Canada's constitutional proclamation in Ottawa, April 17, 1982. (Ron Poling)

Queen Elizabeth is seated next to Prince Philip on thrones from the Senate chamber on Parliament Hill, April 17, 1982, where they took part in proclaiming Canada's independence from Britain.
(Ron Poling)

They dined on consommé, Arctic char, lamb, Manitoba wild rice, zucchini and a maple syrup dessert in a dazzling room at Rideau Hall, the dignified governor general's residence where the Queen has resided during her four-day visit. Nine Armed Forces musicians entertained while they ate.

During a brief delay before the guests began moving through the reception line to curtsy or shake hands with the Queen, Her Majesty joked: "They don't seem very eager." Most of the dignitaries passed quickly through the reception line but some chatted briefly with the Queen, who smiled directly at everyone. Chatting with Jean Wadds, Canada's top diplomat in London, the Queen, in an apparent reference to the Constitution ceremonies, said she had great fun and a marvellous time. To another guest who was concerned because rain began to pour down only moments after the Queen signed the royal proclamation, the Queen remarked: "I was dry." The Queen had been protected by a canopy and umbrellas during the ceremony.

PREMIER DRUNK –
ON DIANA'S CHARMS

ST. ANDREWS, NEW BRUNSWICK, JUNE 20, 1983 (CP) – Prince Charles and Diana, Princess of Wales, continued to attract adoring crowds on the weekend, overshadowing a bit of testiness between New Brunswick Premier Richard Hatfield and the British press.

While British newspapers had a field day at Hatfield's expense – and he took a few shots at them – Charles and Diana and their fans were apparently oblivious to it.

When the couple left for Halifax on a leisurely overnight cruise aboard the yacht *Britannia*, they left behind thousands of happy fans. Today, after a brief stop in the Nova Scotia capital, they leave for Ottawa aboard a Canadian Forces plane.

Diana, Princess of Wales, seated next to Prime Minister Trudeau, chats with Governor General Edward Schreyer during ceremonies on Parliament Hill welcoming the royal couple to Ottawa, June 20, 1983. (Andy Clark)

Hatfield confessed in an interview Sunday that he was drunk on the charms of the princess when he delivered a flowery – some said puzzling – toast to Charles and Diana at a provincial dinner Friday in Saint John. He caused a stir when he said: "We have heard and read

the lies.... It was wonderful to meet and know the truth."

His remarks made headlines in British Sunday newspapers. One referred to him as "a noted eccentric ... also known as Disco Dickie." *The Daily Mail* said the couple was confused by the premier's words, which reporters said were apparently a criticism of gossipy journalism about the royal family.

Asked by reporters whether he was inebriated when he gave the toast, Hatfield said the question was "further evidence of (British reporters') crudity and bad manners."

Charles and Diana's arrival in this pastoral resort town attracted people from the New England states as well as from other parts of New Brunswick. It brought the same emotional response as earlier visits to Saint John and the northern region of the province – squeals and gasps of delight and even tears. A 17-year-old girl, who had waited outside All Saints Anglican Church for six hours before the couple arrived, said afterwards: "I gave him a kiss and then I just started crying."

The church was full and the congregation spilled onto the lawn as Charles read the lesson. Many wished him a happy Father's Day during a walkabout. Although the day is not widely celebrated in Britain, Charles told one child who gave him a card that he had heard of the day. To others who asked what Prince William would receive on his first birthday on Tuesday, Charles replied: "Something he can't break."

After the service, the couple had two walkabouts and attended a reception in this town founded by United Empire Loyalists 200 years ago.

During a weekend stop in Campbellton, the prince received a model canoe and a set of salmon flies. He thought Prince William would enjoy playing with the canoe in his bath, "and even if I have no success with (the flies) in Scotland, I can always play with them in the bath as well."

Prime Minister Pierre Trudeau chats with the Princess of Wales at the head table during a dinner in Ottawa, June 15, 1983. (Andy Clark)

ANTI-ROYALISTS GO TO GROUND FOR CHARLES AND DIANA'S CAPITAL VISIT

The Princess of Wales smiles broadly with a tiara on as she stands in a reception line at Government House just prior to dinner, June 20, 1983. (Ron Poling)

OTTAWA, JUNE 21, 1983 (CP) – The anti-monarchists were in hiding Monday. From commoners to archbishop and legislators, all were effusive in their praise of Prince Charles and Diana, Princess of Wales. Complimentary adjectives were flying from all quarters from the time the royal couple arrived in the national capital Monday afternoon and continued past 11:20 p.m. EDT when they said good night to guests at a state dinner and retired to their rooms at Government House, the Governor General's official residence.

At mid-afternoon, police estimated 25,000 to 30,000 spectators gathered on Parliament Hill in blistering sun for a 30-minute walk-about. Many pushed past barricades and police for a better look at the future king and queen of Canada. But thousands had to be content with a glimpse of her white-feathered hat.

Some who did speak briefly with Diana wished her son William a happy birthday. He is one year old today. "Oh, wow, it was really weird," said Julie Kennedy, 12, of Ottawa. "I've never seen a princess before."

Some endured the heat out of respect for the monarchy. Others, like Bonnie MacDougall of Ottawa, said: "It's fun to see a big-time celebrity like Diana."

The couple attended a private reception for MPs on Parliament Hill who gushed praise for the princess. "She's so beautiful," said Bill Jarvis, Progressive Conservative MP for the Ontario riding of Perth. "I suppose being a princess helps but she is still a beautiful, beautiful woman."

There was another private reception at Government House for four regiments of which the prince is colonel-in-chief. It was the same all over again at the state dinner. Archbishop Joseph Plourde of Ottawa described them as a fine couple. "Even if I am a clergyman I can say that she is a beautiful woman," he added after emerging from the closed dinner.

Roland Michener, former governor general, said: "I enjoyed her company very much. She's a very delightful person indeed."

But there was one fly in the ointment. A crow, actually. Prime Minister Pierre Trudeau, several members of his cabinet and government opposition leaders had to duck out of the state dinner to rush back to the Commons for a vote related to the Crowsnest Pass freight rate.

Diana, Princess of Wales, smiles as a lady shows her a flag with a portrait of her and Prince Charles in Ottawa, June 20, 1983. (Andy Clark)

Princess Diana and Prince charles tour Shelburne, Nova Scotia, 1983. (CP)

DIANA EMBARRASSED AS CHARLES TALKS ABOUT HAVING MORE CHILDREN

ST. JOHN'S, NEWFOUNDLAND, JUNE 24, 1983 (CP) – Thrilling masses wherever he and his young wife went during a full day of functions Thursday, Prince Charles announced a desire for more children to an appreciative crowd, and urged the preservation of the traditional Newfoundland way of life.

The prince drew approving murmurs from the crowd at a youth festival in the morning and provoked a rash of speculation from the travelling British press corps with his comment that he was looking forward to having more children.

His wife Diana, Princess of Wales, could plainly be seen to whisper "so embarrassing" to Reverend James Hickey of Portugal Cove, Newfoundland, who was sitting next to her on the dais when Charles made his comment.

Diana is all smiles after receiving a bouquet of flowers, June 25, 1983, in St. John's. (Andy Clark)

Charles later quipped, "I love embarrassing my wife at least once a day."

The British press contingent used that remark as the peg for a day of speculation, grilling those who had spoken to either Charles or Diana about whether the couple had added anything to Charles's statement. The reference to Prince William and the prospect of a larger family was a high point in a day of official duties for the couple, who also visited a children's hospital in the morning before Charles presented new colours to the Royal Newfoundland Regiment in the afternoon. Diana, who has by far been the biggest drawing card on the tour, took the afternoon off to rest on the yacht, disappointing the crowds lining the motorcade route. As they have at other stops during the 18-day Canadian tour, big crowds came out to see

the royal yacht *Britannia*, and traffic jams have become common in downtown St. John's.

The couple wowed the formally dressed guests at the city's fanciest hotel for a provincial dinner in the evening. Diana provoked the now-standard gapes and gasps when she entered wearing an apricot taffeta gown with Queen Mary's diamond and pearl tiara and the Family Order, a miniature bejewelled picture of the Queen. After being presented with gifts of Newfoundland parkas for the family, Charles made his quiet pitch for preservation of the traditional fishery and outport way of life, a sentiment often expressed by his hosts in the Newfoundland government.

Queen Elizabeth looks behind her after hearing footsteps from a youngster who wanted to present flowers to Her Majesty in Vancouver, March 9, 1983. The girl made her way past security, presented her flowers and left. John Clyne, the Chancellor of the University of British Columbia, was escorting the Queen on campus. (Mike Blake)

The look of joy and a dream come true is mirrored in a little girl's face as she talks to Diana, Princess of Wales, in St. John's, June 23, 1983. The royal couple toured the Janeway Child Health Centre during their stay. (Andy Clark)

QUEEN ENTERTAINED AT HISTORICAL, MULTICULTURAL FESTIVITIES IN THREE PROVINCES

WINNIPEG, OCTOBER 7, 1984 (CP) – With a wave of her familiar gloved hand, the Queen bid farewell to Canada from the ramp of an Royal Air Force jet on Sunday, ending her 14-day visit to three Canadian provinces.

As a band struck up *God Save The Queen*, a military corps fired off a 21-gun salute, marking the end of gruelling tour that had taken her from the coasts of New Brunswick to the small towns of Ontario and finally to the multicultural communities of Manitoba. Hundreds of people gathered in cool, cloudy weather at Canadian Forces Base Winnipeg for one last chance to catch a glimpse of the Queen, who was attired in a mauve-coloured co-ordinated suit with matching beret. Present to bid her farewell officially were Governor General Jeanne Sauvé, Prime Minister Brian Mulroney, and Manitoba Lieutenant-Governor Pearl McGonigal, Premier Howard Pawley and other dignitaries.

The Queen's departure for Lexington, Kentucky, for a private holiday came on the heels of a formal banquet Saturday night where she spoke of the importance of preserving the Commonweath. She toured an aviation museum Sunday, meeting with First World War veterans. One of them, 92-year-old Don McLaren of Vancouver, flew Sopwith Camels in France with the Royal Air Force.

"But these are old, past memories," said McLaren. "Things have grown up big since then, haven't they, eh? All these fine young people coming along…." McLaren paused, looked towards the flags flapping in the breeze and said: "Canada's one of the greatest nations in the Commonwealth."

More tribute was paid to the Commonwealth and the Crown on Saturday night as 1,600 people clinked glasses in a toast to the Queen at a banquet. "No one should think that the continued existence of the

The royal yacht Britannia *carrying Queen Elizabeth and Prince Philip from Victoria, makes her way through Vancouver harbour March 9, 1983, as people line the walkway to catch a glimpse of the vessel. (Nick Didlick)*

Bathtub racers from Nanaimo welcome Queen Elizabeth and Prince Philip who arrived in Nanaimo, March 10, 1983, aboard the Royal Barge. Nanaimo annually hosts the world's largest bathtub race from Nanaimo to Vancouver. (Gerry Kahrmann)

Commonwealth is due to sentiment or nostalgia," said the Queen in an after-dinner speech. "It provides a practical framework for both formal and informal co-operation between governments and institutions without fuss or bother . . . it is just because this takes place with so little fuss that it seldom makes any news."

She also said she was encouraged by the crowds who had come out to welcome her throughout her tour, saying they demonstrated that the symbol of the Crown "still has a real value." The prime minister, who was seated at the Queen's side, drew applause when he said in a speech that the monarchy was a central feature of Canada's national life and vital in preserving world peace. Mulroney added that "many of the factors which inhibit progress would be removed if the resources devoted to preparation for war could be diverted to the requirements of a durable peace."

The Queen began her tour in New Brunswick, where she and Prince Philip spent 2 ½ days attending functions to celebrate that province's 200th birthday. The royal couple made a special point to recognize New Brunswick's bicultural heritage, making their first stop in the Acadian fishing village of Shediac, where French-speaking New Brunswickers clutching Union Jacks gave her a warm welcome.

The Queen and the Prince also celebrated Ontario's bicentennial, spending nine days in a province where United Empire Loyalists settled during the aftermath of the American Revolution. Thousands of people, many of them Americans, came out to see the royal couple as they visited Ottawa, several communities along the St. Lawrence River, Toronto, Windsor, Brantford and Sudbury.

In Manitoba, the Queen toured alone while Prince Philip returned to London. One of the highlights of four-day visit was a tour of the Ukrainian community of Dauphin, Manitoba. There she dined on traditional Ukrainian food and watched as horsemen dressed as

Prince Philip leans over to kiss Queen Elizabeth goodbye at Sudbury airport, October 4, 1984. (Tim Clark)

Queen Elizabeth arrives in Moncton, September 24, 1984 for a two-week visit to Canada.(Fred Chartrand)

Ukrainian Cossacks thundered across the plains to welcome her. She also received a warm welcome in St. Boniface, a predominately French-speaking area of Winnipeg, where a brigade of canoeists representing voyageurs re-enacted the landing of explorer Pierre LaVerendrye. The Queen's visit to Manitoba was held to commemorate LaVerendrye's Manitoba expedition 250 years ago.

Some of the most memorable events during the royal stay in Canada didn't happen here but in the pages of the Fleet Street newspapers back in Britain, where outraged reports of Ontario Transport Minister James Snow annoying the Queen by touching her on the back and arm were splashed about. Snow said later he doubted the apparent breach of protocol ever happened. He said he received a private communication from the Queen's party expressing her "complete displeasure with the allegations" and assuring the minister that reports she was upset were unfounded.

The British tabloids had a field day again a few days later when Toronto newspapers published stories describing the 58-year-old Queen as looking bored, dowdy, tired and given to wearing unflattering clothes.

"Astonishing attack on the Queen," said a front-page headline in *The Daily Express*. "Amazing attack on the bored Queen," said the rival *Daily Mail*. British fashion commentators jumped to her defence, saying her conservative style of dress was appropriate for her age and position. "She isn't a fashion plate — she is a monarch," said Freddie Fox, who has made the Queen's hats for 13 years. "You can't have both."

– by Nelle Oosterom

Residents of Cardinal, Ontario, wave to Queen Elizabeth and Prince Philip as the royal train takes them through eastern Ontario, September 27, 1984, during their visit to Canada. (Fred Chartrand)

HECTIC VISIT TO BRITISH COLUMBIA TAKES TOLL ON DIANA

VANCOUVER, MAY 8, 1986 (CP) – A week-long royal tour, a regal christening of a world's exposition, and a fainting princess served to endear the Prince and Princess of Wales to hundreds of thousands of British Columbians.

In the longest visit ever by any member of the Royal Family to a single province, Charles and Diana made their first joint visit to British Columbia, opened the world's exposition on transportation and communication, and toured several Interior B.C. communities. While the pace of visits to Victoria, Vancouver, Kelowna, Kamloops, Nanaimo and Prince George may have served to satisfy the public's royal curiosity, Diana finally felt the effects during a hectic tour of five pavilions Tuesday at the world's fair. Under warm sunshine, one of the few solar indulgences in a week of dark skies and sometimes driving rain, Diana was touring the California pavilion when she had a dizzy spell. She rested briefly and resumed her schedule while a royal spokesman hastily told reporters the Princess of Wales was tired but not pregnant.

A few hours later, Charles teased an audience at a dinner, telling the gathering that Diana was "about to have sextuplets, which is really why she fainted." While the audience was still trying to grasp his statement, he countered with: "It's not actually true."

The reason for the royal visit was to officially open Expo 86, the $1.6-billion, 5 ½-month world's fair that was conceived and financed to a large extent by the B.C. government. While Diana's fainting spell and the

Diana, Princess of Wales, in Burnaby, May 6, 1986. (Ryan Remiorz)

royal visit itself served as excellent publicity for the fair, the prince added his endorsement in a brief speech at the Plaza of Nations that concluded the visit. "I hope very much that this Expo will be the success that it deserves to be because so many people have put so much time and effort and dedication into achieving this particular project," Charles said.

B.C. Premier Bill Bennett lauded the couple because they had "conquered" the hearts of British Columbians. The visit confirmed the popularity of the royal couple, especially Diana, who was in British Columbia for the first time and who seemed to be the most sought after by crowds at every stop.

The couple made three separate trips to the main Expo site on False Creek. They also toured the smaller site on Burrard Inlet, home of the most expensive – and permanent – Canadian pavilion that will become a trade and convention centre after the fair ends October 13. There were galas, dinners and even a rock concert with

Diana, Princess of Wales, mingles with the crowd gathered to welcome her and Prince Charles outside the parliament buildings in Victoria, April 30, 1986. (CP)

Bryan Adams, Sheena Easton and other performers at the Expo Theatre.

The couple's last day, prior to the final Expo engagement, was spent in more familiar duties – Charles spent time talking to some former street youths while Diana visited Children's Hospital. A former day-care attendant, Diana was at ease talking to children, some of whom are battling cancer. In another part of the city, Charles chatted with bingo-playing seniors and then spent about 20 minutes talking to a group of youths in a program that takes them away from drugs, prostitution and street life.

– *by Greg Joyce*

The Princess of Wales during a brief visit to Kelowna, May 3, 1986. (Ron Poling)

PRINCESS ANNE DEMONSTRATES GOOD AIM ON FIRING RANGE

OROMOCTO, NEW BRUNSWICK, JUNE 26, 1986 (CP) – Princess Anne continued to score points as she ended her week-long visit to Canada on Thursday. She was warmly welcomed by crowds throughout her three-day visit to New Brunswick, and here at Canadian Forces Base Gagetown, she managed a bull's eye on the firing range as she demolished an old truck with a well-aimed cannon blast.

The slim, 35-year-old princess sauntered onto the firing range dressed in drab, olive-green fatigues complemented by polished, black combat boots. Her long hair was swept up and knotted at the back, but a few wisps escaped in the strong, chilly wind that whipped across the open fields. She nimbly clambered over military training and recon-

Queen Elizabeth listens to Prime Minister Pierre Trudeau at a ceremony in Vancouver in 1983, inviting people to Expo 86. (CP)

naissance vehicles with the sure-footedness of a veteran tank commander. She laughingly scorned a soldier's offered hand of help as she jumped off a Cougar tank-training vehicle, saying: "Come on, I don't spend my life sitting in chairs, you know."

The princess flattened an army truck parked on the range for target practice with her second shot from the 76-millimetre cannon perched on the front of the armoured Cougar. "It's burning now," the somewhat surprised-looking princess told one of the officers as flames and black smoke engulfed the truck. There was an enthusiastic round of applause from military personnel and dignitaries gathered at the site.

Princess Anne was invited to Gagetown, one of the largest military training bases in the

Commonwealth, in her capacity as colonel-in-chief of the 8th Canadian Hussars, a venerable cavalry regiment that traces its origins back to 1775.

In her address to the Hussars, of which she has been colonel-in-chief since 1972, she engaged in a bit of gentle humour, poking fun at the regiment's emphasis on athletic prowess. "I am mildly concerned that as a cavalry regiment it has taken to jumping out of airplanes, with its vehicles, and into Goose Bay and gaining a reputation for physical fitness and athletic excellence that seems completely out of character for a cavalry regiment," she said. "But I have no doubt it has frightened your friends so goodness knows what it has done to your potential enemies."

Her review of the regiment, for which she donned a buttercup yellow suit, capped a low-key, six-day royal visit to Alberta, Ontario and New Brunswick. While she failed to attract the huge crowds that show up for Prince Charles and Diana, she nevertheless had good-sized turnouts at most of her stops. She was friendly, if a bit aloof, with the people she met and managed to dispel the "Princess Grump" image that has haunted her from earlier years.

Earlier in the day, the princess toured the bioengi-neering institute at the University of New Brunswick, where electronically controlled, artificial limbs are made and tested. She charmed nine-year-old Sara Kerr of Hampton, New Brunswick, who was invited to meet the princess and show off her myoelectric arm. The little girl was born without a left hand and for the past five years has used a specially fitted myoelectric hand that looks much like the real thing and has some of the same functions. Kerr showed the princess how she can open and close her fist and told her how the artificial limb attached just above the elbow lets her to do many things that had been impossible.

"I can play on the monkey bars at the playground and I can climb stuff and use it for swinging," she said.

The battery-powered arm has electrodes in its socket that fit over Kerr's stump, touching the surface of her skin. The electrodes pick up and amplify muscle signals, telling the hand to open or close. Jim Kerr said the artificial arm has given his daughter a more normal life.

"I would think most of the kids in her class and most of the kids in the neighborhood don't realize she only has one arm," he said. "So it's a big plus for her that way."

– by Chris Morris

NERVOUS AWARD-WINNER CAN ONLY STARE AT QUEEN MUM'S JEWELRY

MONTREAL, JUNE 5, 1987 (CP) – Linda and Patrick Blouin were nervously holding hands in the back seat of their parents' car Friday when they began to think the traffic jam would never end. After completing a three-year program of community work and proving their physical and academic mettle, the brother and sister were about to receive gold Duke of Edinburgh awards from the Queen Mother – if they could make it through the traffic to the Black Watch armoury.

"We began to think about getting out of the car and walking, but then my father found a short cut and we got there on time," said Linda Blouin, 21. The two, along with 52 other young people from Quebec, Ontario, New Brunswick and Nova Scotia, were presented with the awards by the Queen Mother before about 200 friends and family members.

By the time her name was called to receive the award, Blouin thought she might be too nerve-racked to move. "I finally got up there and I couldn't do anything except stare at her jewelry," she said.

Patrick Blouin followed his sister, and he said the Queen Mother congratulated him and asked what he had done to receive the award. Blouin, 18, a budding chef, served breakfast and dinners to a regiment on patrol as part of his fulfilment of the program's requirements. After the hour-long ceremony, the Queen Mother attended a private reception given by Premier Robert Bourassa.

Earlier in the day, about 200 people, many of them elderly, slipped through police lines in front of the Ritz-Carlton hotel and rushed

The Queen Mother (previous page) waves to the crowd at the Queen's Plate in Toronto, July 14, 1985. (Mike Blake)

*Her Majesty the Queen
Mother views the city of
Montreal from the lookout
atop Mount Royal during
a walkabout, June 7, 1987.
(Ryan Remiorz)*

the Queen Mother's limousine. While the incident drew the attention of several policemen who tried to hold back the admirers, the Queen Mother, 86, emerged from the car smiling and waved before entering the hotel where the federal government held a luncheon on her behalf.

Several of the people who rushed were elderly women who had to elbow past a crowd of photographers who were covering the royal visit. Many of them were angered by the fact that the media blocked their view of the Queen Mother.

"I'm not angry, I'm just disturbed," said one woman, who refused to identify herself. "All you people come and stand in front of me and show me your cards and I don't see anything."

The Queen Mother is in Montreal as part of a four-day visit for the 125th anniversary of the Black Watch regiment, of which she is colonel-in-chief.   —by Robert Russo

The Queen Mother is greeted by Governor General Jeanne Sauvé, Prime Minister Brian Mulroney and his wife Mila, at Uplands Airbase in Ottawa, June 4, 1987. (Fred Chartrand)

YORKS CELEBRATE FIRST ANNIVERSARY AT BUFFALO SLAUGHTER GROUND

HEAD-SMASHED-IN BUFFALO JUMP, ALBERTA, JULY 24, 1987 (CP) – The Duke and Duchess of York passed part of their first anniversary on a prairie hillside that served for thousands of years as a slaughter ground for buffalo.

It was another work day in their tour of Canada. They opened a new provincial tourist centre at the Head-Smashed-In Buffalo Jump, an ancient Indian hunting site on the high plains of southwestern Alberta. And they shared the day with a crowd. About 3,000 people shouted Happy Anniversary and squealed like fans at a Beatles concert as Andrew made a short speech, describing the site as one "for the whole world to come and see."

The romance was mostly in the history and the panorama. Solemn elders from the Blood and Peigan

The Duke and Duchess of York arrive at Ontario historic site Fort William in Thunder Bay, aboard a voyageur canoe, July 16, 1987. The royal couple helped in the paddling for part of the short voyage. (Dave Buston)

Indian nations invoked prayers. Two scarlet-clad Mounties stood guard. A Canadian flag and a Union Jack fluttered over a tepee village. The olive- and tan-coloured prairie stretched more than 20 kilometres beyond toward a hazy horizon.

But Sarah, her hair twisted into a long braid and decorated with a purple ribbon, injected a touch of private romance too. She wore the frock she had on the day she and Andrew sailed off for their private honeymoon last year.

The buffalo jump is an 11-metre-high cliffside where generations of Indians herded bison over the edge to a quick death. One of the largest and most-used sites of its kind, the United Nations recognized it in 1981 as a world heritage site. The $10-million interpretive centre, a kind

Sarah Ferguson, Duchess of York (previous page), looks radiant at a dinner for the royal couple at the Royal York Hotel in Toronto, July 16, 1987. (CP)

Sarah during a canoe trip with her husband in the Northwest Territories, July 28, 1987. (Dave Buston)

of massive educational display, is built of sandstone laid into the hillside and covered with sod to blend in with the surrounding prairie.

Bryan Yellow Horn, a Peigan who co-ordinated the Indian contribution to the centre, said he hopes it will "make the public more aware of our lifestyle in the past and . . . aware of how we are living today." Tourists are welcome, he said.

Harry Shade, 73, a Blood elder, said a prayer during the welcome ceremony but accepted the construction reluctantly. He said Indians here honour the site, which he described as one of the most important buffalo jumps on Alberta's southern plains. "They often come here and pray. They have a contact with the spiritual world. I would rather not have (this) and have the buffalo here, and people come and pray."

The duke and duchess began their day at another major Alberta tourist attraction, a rodeo. They rode a horse-drawn open landau into the arena of the Medicine Hat Stampede and, after a brief welcome that saw the couple laughing and joking with each other, walked up to the grandstand to watch a wild horse race, saddle-bronco riding and steer wrestling.

Sarah wore an emerald green suede jacket and a classic cowgirl skirt. She had been wearing matching green boots when she arrived in Medicine Hat but had switched to tan boots for the rodeo an hour later. Andrew walked into a civic lunch wearing a plain grey suit but sported a western-style jacket and bolo tie by the time he reached the rodeo ground.

Clusters of about 100 people gathered at the Medicine Hat and Fort Macleod airports to see the couple as they toured southern Alberta. Dozens more lined rural roads, some waiting for the royal motorcade with heart-decked signs reading Happy Anniversary Sarah and Andrew. The couple traveled to Edmonton to tour a reconstructed fur-trading post, followed by a state dinner. They will move north to Grande Prairie, Alberta, and Yellowknife on Saturday. From Yellowknife they will leave Monday for a private week-long canoe trip in the Territories before returning to Britain.

–by Mark Lisac

The Duke and Duchess of York wave to photographers from atop the tour boat Maid of the Mist *during their visit to Niagara Falls, July 18, 1987. (Dave Buston)*

DUKE REDUCES TEENS TO GIGGLES
AT AWARDS DINNER

TORONTO, MARCH 14, 1989 (CP) – When they encountered royalty unexpectedly for the first time, the four teenagers dressed in crisp school uniforms giggled and blushed hotly.

"I didn't know what to say," Elizabeth Wilson, 18, said Monday after bumping into Prince Philip at a downtown hotel. "I didn't think he was going to stop."

But the prince, guest of honour at a fundraising dinner for the Duke of Edinburgh Awards, did stop to chat with Wilson and three of her classmates on his way into a posh banquet hall for a gourmet meal. About 860 people who attended the $250-a-plate event formed a sea of black and white tuxedoes and beaded dresses.

The awards, sponsored by the prince, were introduced in 1963 to encourage perseverance, initiative and community responsibility. More than 100,000 young people between the ages of 14 and 25 have participated in the program.

"This is the other half of the educational experience – discovering what life is really like. It's a kind of do-it-yourself development kit," Prince Philip said of the program after the meal.

Program participants set goals for themselves in four areas: voluntary service, skill development, physical recreation and expeditions. Those who achieve their goals receive a medal and a certificate.

During his brief speech, the prince entertained the audience with anecdotes of the awards' evolution. At first, girls were not

Prince Philip launches the World Wildlife Fund's Duke Edinburgh Fund during a news conference in Toronto, October 20, 2001. (J.P. Moczulski)

required to fulfill fitness requirements, but were given a homemaking section instead.

"I thought I was being modern about this. Until about 20 years later, we were hauled up in front of the equal opportunities commission and told we were discriminating against the girls," the prince said. "So it just shows you can't win. Not with women, anyway!"

The awards program has spread to about 50 countries – including Jordan and Israel – and the prince said he hoped it would affect more than the youth of those countries. "You never know. It may help people talk to each other across the border."

– by Wendy Cox

Queen Elizabeth chats with chiefs of Treaty 7 on her visit to Spruce Meadows near Calgary, June 29, 1990. The Queen was presented with a petition asking for her help in their fight for self government. (Dave Buston)

The Queen is greeted by pro-independence supporters as she arrives at a park in Hull, Quebec, for Canada Day celebrations, July 1, 1990. (Ryan Remiorz)

QUEEN MOTHER INSISTS ON SEEING SKYDOME DURING ANNIVERSARY TOUR

TORONTO, JULY 9, 1989 (CP) – Two favourites carried the day at the Queen's Plate when the Queen Mother conquered the crowd and With Approval took the trophy.

Arriving on the track at Woodbine raceway for the 130th running of the colourful event in a stately horse-drawn landau, the regal royal paused, on cue, to wave at the 32,485 cheering fans dressed in their racing finery. For her last official appearance on a visit that ends when she returns to London today, the Queen Mother wore a floral print silk dress of white, pink and grey with matching chiffon coat and a pink straw hat with an upturned brim. Jockey Don Seymour, riding Kinghaven Farms' With Approval to a photo finish over Most Valiant, was dressed in the navy blue and white silks of the owner's colors.

The Queen Mother inspects the Guard of Honour, after arriving on Parliament Hill, July 5, 1989. (Ron Poling)

Just prior to the title race – the seventh she has attended at Woodbine – the Queen Mother mingled with fashionably dressed invited guests in the walking ring to view the horses entered for the $257,660 winner's purse. So many people jockeyed for a personal greeting, including hockey czar Harold Ballard and his companion Yolanda Ballard, that the Queen Mother had difficulty seeing the horses.

"She's gorgeous," Harold Ballard said of the 88-year-old smiling matriarch, his senior by just three years and five days.

The race was the climax of the last day in the Queen Mother's Canadian tour, which began with a splash of excitement for her security guards when someone threw an egg from the roof of a house across from St. Mary

Magdalene's church. Although it was not a direct hit – the Queen Mother was already inside – RCMP officers, a reporter and a media relations co-ordinator got sprayed with yolk. Officers jumped metal barricades in a futile search for the culprit.

Later, the Queen Mother unveiled a plaque to the late Canadian composer Healey Willan, the former organist at the church, which was celebrating its 100th anniversary. Before the Queen's Plate, she attended a private luncheon at the residence of food magnate Galen Weston, where she has been staying during her five-day visit.

The highlight of the visit occurred Saturday, when the "Queen Mum," as she is affectionately nicknamed, took her itinerary into her own hands to make an unscheduled visit to the SkyDome. It appeared to be a welcome break from official engagements – luncheons, teas, dedications and unveilings – designed to mark the 50th anniversary of her first visit to Canada, the 1939 royal tour with her husband King George VI, who died in 1952.

Security and stadium officials hastily obliged on only a few hours notice when the Queen Mother gently insisted she be allowed to see the domed stadium, which she had mentioned Thursday in a speech written by Ontario government staff. Appearing lively and interested in its engineering, the Queen Mother quizzed Stadium Corp. executive Bob Hunter on the way the artificial turf is rolled up and on the dome's acoustics and size. She expressed regrets at not being able to see a baseball game or concert. "That would have been fun."

Earlier Saturday, the Queen Mother met officers of her Canadian regiments, the Toronto Scottish, Black Watch of Canada and the Canadian Armed Forces Medical Services, at Fort York armoury. On Friday, she won the hearts of veterans and hundreds of people lining her well-publicized route in London, Ontario, as she exchanged a yellow freesia from her bouquet for a rose, made a well-timed save as one man lost his grip on his cane, and posed patiently for pictures.

The rose came from Wilf Jordan, 68, a veteran and resident at Parkwood Hospital, who got a freesia back for his granddaughter Kerrie Sobie. "What other monarch will you ever get to do that?" he asked, his blue eyes twinkling beneath the beret of the Canadian Army Service Corps.

The sentiment was shared by many of those who waited for hours, often in blistering heat, to catch a

glimpse of the most popular member of the Royal Family as she attended a luncheon Thursday at Toronto's King Edward Hotel and a welcoming ceremony at the Ontario legislature. Many feared it would be their last opportunity to see the Queen Mother, since she celebrates her 89th birthday in less than a month.

"She's an example to all of us and personifies everything good and loving," British-born Terry Penedel, 50, said as she waited outside the hotel. "At 88, we may never see her again."

But the Queen Mother, who has said she plans to live to 100 so that she can receive a telegram of congratulations from her daughter the Queen, appeared to welcome several invitations to return to Canada. She laughed with the congregation Sunday when Reverend Harold Nahabedian welcomed her. "As I look around I cannot see an empty seat," the minister told her. "May I say I hope Your Majesty will come back."

– by Laura Eggertson

The Queen Mother waves to cheering crowds as she passes in the landau on Parliament Hill, July 5, 1989, while a Mountie watches in the background. (Ron Poling)

PRINCE HARRY'S FIRST FOREIGN WALKABOUT

NIAGARA FALLS, ONTARIO, OCTOBER 26, 1991 (CP) – Prince Harry, the fair-haired seven-year-old who's third in line to the throne, learned the ropes of his trade today during his first official walkabout abroad. With his beaming mother Diana, Princess of Wales, looking on, the little boy shook hands with delighted fans before the spectacular scenery of Niagara Falls.

"He had a little boy's handshake. It was natural – just what you would expect," said a thrilled Nicole Marsden, 30, of Burlington, Ontario. She described the little prince's demeanor as "shy and mischievous."

Harry and his nine-year-old brother William were joined by their mother for the threesome's first public appearance in Canada together since the family arrived for an official visit Wednesday. Donning royal blue rain slickers, they viewed the falls from the famous *Maid of the Mist* tour boat. Charles spent the day with Ontario business leaders.

The night before, the Prince of Wales supped with military in a Fort York armoury mess, while the princess stepped out for a night on the town. Dressed in a white, decolletage cocktail dress under a black jacket, Diana arrived at the Royal Alexandra Theatre for a performance of the long-running musical *Les Miserables*. It was expected she would be escorted by eldest son William, but a spokesman for the princess said Diana decided at the last minute to leave him on the royal yacht *Britannia* to allow him a good night's sleep before their helicopter flight to Niagara. "He's not coming now," said the spokesman who cited rules of royal protocol in refusing to be identified. "They wouldn't have got back to the yacht until at least

Diana, Princess of Wales, listens to a speech in the Science North Center in Sudbury, October 24, 1991. (Bill Becker)

11:30 and she decided she didn't want to tire him out."

The boys spent Friday at Science North in the northern Ontario city of Sudbury, where their parents were entertained the day before. Accompanied by security guards and their nanny, the boys – dressed casually in blue jeans, denim shirts and sneakers – arrived at noon practically unnoticed by most other visitors to the centre. Alan Nursall, the centre's program director, said Harry described the exhibits, which include a giant piano keyboard built into the ground and strength testing devices, as "brilliant."

Meanwhile in Toronto, Charles donned full military dress Friday evening to tour the armoury after spending the day enchanting all he encountered. The charming prince made a fairytale come true for a would-be Cinderella when he stooped to put on her missing shoe. Charles made the gallant gesture when Karen Haslam, Ontario's culture minister, accidentally slipped her left foot out of her shoe while escorting the prince through the doors to the Art Gallery of Ontario.

"I said: 'My gracious, my prince is handing me my shoe,'" Haslam said later. "And he said: 'Thank goodness it fits.'"

It was one of several warm moments that seemed to melt the cool facade of a prince who is often overshadowed by his wife. Diana, appearing in various brightly colored, tailored jackets and skirts, has captured most of the attention since the couple arrived in Toronto on Wednesday.

On Friday, Diana comforted AIDS patients at Toronto's Casey House. Sitting on a radiator, she placed herself next to Wayne Taylor, a 27-year-old patient at the hospice who handed her a sweatshirt wrapped in a red bow.

"Her Royal Highness was so gracious, so warm, so gentle, so caring," hospital spokesman Jim Wakeford said after she left to visit patients at a rehabilitation centre. "It was just one of the most moving experiences I've ever had. She not only knows the illness, she knows its indignities."

Charles did some charming of his own, returning a hearty hug from a woman waiting to greet him at the art gallery and amusing a gathering of the Law Society of Upper Canada. After being made an honorary bencher of the society that governs Ontario lawyers, the prince imagined out loud how he and his family

Prince Charles and Diana, Princess of Wales, with their sons Prince William (left) and Prince Harry, bid goodbye to a cheering Toronto crowd from aboard the royal yacht Brittania, *October 27, 1991. (Hans Deryk)*

might put their stack of honorary law degrees to use.

"Between us all we could boast a positive faculty of law graduates. We could start a practice operating from a particularly salubrious office block in central London – a move which would send shivers down the spines of countless law societies throughout the Commonwealth," he quipped. The dark-suited prince was in a particularly jocular mood as he became the fifth member of the Royal Family and third Prince of Wales to be honoured by the society. "We could litigate and mitigate – expostulate and adumbrate. Perhaps, ladies and gentlemen, even titillate," he told an audience that included former federal Liberal leader John Turner, Ontario Premier Bob Rae, and Charles Dubin, Ontario's chief justice.

Earlier Friday, the royal couple, in one of their rare moments together, wowed tens of thousands of admirers at city hall during a walk through Nathan Philips Square. In the evening, Canada's rich and powerful came out to a splashy, black-tie affair to raise money for literacy, where Diana dazzled the 800 guests with her floor-length gown with an emerald off-the-shoulder bodice made of silk. The famous Queen Mary tiara, the diamond and pearl drop headdress given to the princess as a wedding gift by Queen Elizabeth, sparkled from her golden tresses.   – by Wendy McCann

Diana, Princess of Wales, arrives at the Royal York Hotel for an evening gala, October 26, 1991. (Hans Deryk)

QUEEN CELEBRATES COUNTRY'S 125TH BIRTHDAY WITH CANADIANS

Queen Elizabeth (previous page) walks around a statue that depicts her riding her horse Centennial, shortly after she unveiled it on Parliament Hill, June 30, 1992. (Ron Poling)

Queen Elizabeth cuts into a giant birthday cake as Prime Minister Brian Mulroney looks on during celebrations in Ottawa, July 1, 1992. (Chuck Mitchell)

OTTAWA, JULY 1, 1992 (CP) – Queen and country were feted with flags, flypasts and fireworks on a Canada Day in which patriotism got louder cheers than politics. The tens of thousands who packed Parliament Hill and the surrounding streets for a daylong 125th birthday celebration came for a party, not politics. They made that clear with lukewarm applause for national unity appeals from the Queen and Prime Minister Brian Mulroney.

But the patriotism came through with prolonged clapping and cheers as the Queen paid tribute to Canadian soldiers serving as peacekeepers in the war-torn cities of what once was Yugoslavia. "I want to say a special word about the brave Canadian soldiers who today seek to bring peace under UN auspices…." That was as far as she got in her first

try as the crowd drowned her with cheers. "As Queen of Canada, I salute their contribution with pride," she concluded, to more applause in her noon-hour Canada Day speech.

In the evening, there were loud cheers for Quebec pop star Celine Dion, who added her plea for unity in a satellite broadcast from Seville, Spain, where she is appearing at Expo 92. "I'm against separation," she said. "The most important thing is to respect each other's cultures."

Mulroney got a few scattered boos as he rose for a brief unity plug at the noon ceremonies. He quoted Sir John A. Macdonald, who warned that Canada would sink into insignificance if it allowed its unity to be broken. "Let me tell you today, Your Majesty, that we shall not suffer Canada to be broken," he

said. "We shall fight for Canada and her unity by all democratic means and we shall win."

The Queen, too, spoke for unity, urging politicians to put the national interest first in their deliberations. "They will, I know, spare no effort in their pursuit of the success expected of them." Although the Queen works on her own speeches, such digressions into the political realm are approved by the Prime Minister's Office.

The noon celebration featured the usual ceremonial trappings. The Queen arrived in an open carriage escorted by Mounties with 125th birthday pennons on their lances. She was welcomed by Governor General Ray Hnatyshyn, who told her: "Your Majesty, Canada is and continues to be a country to make you proud." Hnatyshyn spoke a few words in Inuktitut, in tribute to Aboriginal Peoples.

Artillery boomed out salutes that sent echoes

Queen Elizabeth smiles as she chats with Major Luc-Andre Racine, commander of a guard of honour made up of members of the Royal 22nd Regiment during an inspection on Parliament Hill, June 30, 1992. (Ron Poling)

Queen Elizabeth inspects the Ceremonial Guard on Parliament Hill, during Canada Day celebrations, July 1, 1992. (Fred Chartrand)

chasing themselves among the Parliament Buildings and which, after a prolonged birthday cannonade, almost darkened the Hill under a pall of powder smoke. Three CF-18 jets screamed low overhead, followed 30 minutes later by the Tutor jets of the Snowbirds aerial acrobatic team.

O Canada rang out from thousands of throats that almost drowned themselves out in the peculiar reverberations from the surrounding stone buildings. A televised show included musical groups like Prairie Oyster and the Rankin Family as well as ethnic dancers and several choirs. The Queen whisked away by motorcade to a Rideau Hall lunch with holders of various national honours and later greeted children at a youth festival in a local park.

Earlier in the day, she had attended a ceremony at Rideau Hall that saw a broad mix of Canadians – including for the first time non-politicians such as hockey great

Prince Andrew chats with students from Lakefield College in Lakefield, September 26, 1992. The prince was on hand to start a cross-country race as part of the college's homecoming and kick-off a fundraiser to build a new resource centre. (Hans Deryk)

Maurice Richard, painter Alex Colville and author W.O. Mitchell – sworn into the Privy Council.

She returned to the Hill for an evening party that tugged at the heartstrings. Olympic champions, retired hockey great Yvan Cournoyer, Anne Murray, Quebec pop star Roch Voisine, actress Tantoo Cardinal, astronaut Roberta Bondar and musician David Foster all swelled the national pride. Gordon Lightfoot's haunting *Canadian Railway Trilogy* was received with reverent attention and then wild applause. The evening ended with gasps and whoops as spectacular multi-colored fireballs and whiz-bang rockets lit up the sky in a fireworks extravaganza.

It was a day when the Maple Leaf fluttered everywhere; tucked into ponytails, painted on foreheads, emblazoned on T-shirts, taped to wheelchairs. It was a day for music. Downtown Ottawa was a cacophony of styles and tempos. Pipers competed with driving rock booming from a giant stage in front of the Peace Tower. Jazz echoed down the Sparks Street Mall and duelled with twanging guitars, lilting fiddles and even the eerie tones of a bandura, a 55-string folk instrument from Ukraine.

— *by John Ward*

QUEEN GREETS CREW WHO RE-ENACTED CABOT'S JOURNEY TO NORTH AMERICA

BONAVISTA, NEWFOUNDLAND, JUNE 24, 1997 (CP) – The weather was nasty enough to make even the heartiest explorer turn back for open water, but the *Matthew* and its crew stuck to the plan Tuesday and completed a 20th-century version of John Cabot's trans-Atlantic voyage.

The wooden square-rigger rolled over rough waves into Bonavista harbour while about 30,000 chilled and wet spectators cheered and waved. The arrival was the centrepiece of Newfoundland's year-long Cabot 500 celebrations marking the European explorer's arrival in North America in 1497. Although the aboriginals and Vikings preceded him, Cabot's journey opened North America to British settlement and trade.

The crew, dressed in 15th-century costumes, appeared delighted to reach terra firma. "It felt fantastic, a great relief," said Capt. David Alan-Williams of Lymington, Britain.

Queen Elizabeth offers a toast to Prime Minister Jean Chrétien during a state dinner in Toronto, June 28, 1997. (Frank Gunn)

Following a welcome that included singing, dancing and greetings from the Queen, Alan-Williams marvelled how the *Matthew* held up in the fierce North Atlantic. "It's just amazing what (Cabot) did. No lighthouses, very little safety equipment and terrible clothing." The *Matthew* was equipped with satellite navigation equipment and other safety-related devices. Everything else about the voyage was meant to be as it was in Cabot's time.

The Queen, who attended the festivities with Prince Philip as part of a 10-day Canadian visit, said Newfoundland became the link between the old and new worlds.

"It represents the geographical and intellectual beginning of modern North America," the Queen remarked, "that extraordinary relationship that has existed between Great Britain and Newfoundland ever since."

Not everyone saw the day quite that way. Aboriginal protesters caught the Queen's attention earlier in the day but did not disrupt her schedule as organizers had feared. They say the celebrations are an insult because they overlook the fact the Beothuk Indians who lived in Newfoundland were exterminated by disease and clashes with the English settlers who followed Cabot. The group of 40 protesters, led by Ovide Mercredi, chief of the Assembly of First Nations, peacefully held placards denouncing the festivities. Mercredi said the estimated $5 million the provincial and federal governments spent on the day's events could be better used to help improve the living conditions of aboriginal people.

The Queen stopped to listen to their native drums and chanting after planting a small tree Bonavista – one of the oldest settlements in North America.

The next day, when the Queen made her first visit to Labrador, she received mixed greetings in the Innu community of Sheshatshiu. About 30 Innu protesters waved placards denouncing her visit while, at the same time, about 350 others welcomed her.

The Queen visited a traditional hunting tent lined with spruce branches and caribou skins. She greeted elders and children dressed in traditional clothes, while wild duck roasted on the stove. Paul Rich, chief of the local Innu band, explained a gift of artwork to the Queen while at the same time making her aware of the problems aboriginals have faced since colonization.

David Alan-Williams, captain of the Matthew, *flanked by Prince Phillip (left), Queen Elizabeth and Newfoundland Premier Brian Tobin (right), shows off the vessel at dockside during the Cabot 500 festivities in Bonavista, June 24, 1997. (Andrew Vaughan)*

"We did not choose to live under someone's laws ... to have our people fall into substance abuse, to be marginalized and to have major mining developments disrupt our way of life," said Rich. He said the Innu's fight is with the Canadian and Newfoundland governments, not the Queen.

Daniel Ashini, vice-president of the Innu Nation and organizer of the protest, said the Queen should support Aboriginal Peoples' right to self-government.

Many who gathered seemed thrilled to see the Queen. "The way I see it, she is everybody's Queen," said Mary Pia Benuen. "It's nice for her to know who the Innu are and why we're fighting for our land claim and self-government all the time."

The Queen's visit to this riverside community of 1,200 stood out on other levels. Dogs meandered about her sand-covered route, and there was not a Union Jack or Maple Leaf in sight. There was none of the gushing witnessed at previous events this week, but there was still a genuine warmth about the event. The community has spent the last several weeks cleaning up along highways and had blue and white balloons tied to a bridge along the road into town.

– *by Michelle MacAfee*

Queen Elizabeth looks on as jockey Mike Smith celebrates his victory aboard Awesome Again in the 138th running of the Queen's Plate at Woodbine racetrack in Toronto, June 29, 1997. (Kevin Frayer)

Queen Elizabeth waves to supporters as she walks off the stage with Prime Minister Jean Chrétien following Canada Day ceremonies in Ottawa, July 1, 1992. (Tom Hanson)

WILLIAM-MANIA HITS B.C. AS ADORING TEENS CROWD YOUNG PRINCE

WHISTLER, BRITISH COLUMBIA, MARCH 29. 1998 (CP) – Prince William will have lots to tell his school chums about his trip to Vancouver and a four-day ski vacation that left no doubt about his popularity with the girls.

There were snowball fights, snowboarding and a ride to a mountain cabin for dinner with his 13-year-old brother Harry and father Prince Charles. "They have had a good holiday – it has been a good time," a palace spokeswoman said as the three royals squeezed in a last bit of skiing. Officials have said it's too soon to say if the royal trio will return to Whistler for another vacation. But it's clear this visit was a lot more than fun.

William, 15, became the object of adoration for screaming teenage girls – a frenzy that surprised some observers of the Royal Family. Some girls followed William from stop to stop during a 24-hour official visit in Vancouver before the royal party headed for Whistler. They bought roses, tulips and teddy bears, then waited hours to hand them to William. Some travelled to Whistler to look for him on the slopes. They flashed homemade signs with such slogans as "William. It's Me You've Been Looking For." They were so serious and earnest that the experience was probably a bit unsettling for the young royal, widely described as deeply uneasy about being a public figure.

"Prince William should know his future wife," said 14-year-old Shannon Raimondo, explaining why she wanted to meet the prince.

He didn't look too happy about meeting

Prince William (left), Prince Charles (centre) and Prince Harry (right) are all smiles as they pause for a picture on the slopes of Whistler Mountain, March 26, 1998. (Frank Gunn)

anyone at first. When William arrived in Vancouver, he walked, head bowed, past hordes of teens into a waterfront hotel. "I'm going to be sick," said a shaky Jessica Larochelle, stricken that her heartthrob had snubbed her.

Prince Harry, 13, appeared to find the mania over his big brother amusing and was more inclined to greet the crowds.

Startled British reporters described the William-mania as a landmark development for the House of Windsor. They knew many British teen girls had a crush on the eldest son of Charles and the late Diana. One London magazine managed to give away 250,000 I Love Willy stickers. But Will-mania exploded in Vancouver.

William eventually became bolder on the trip, grinning as he shook hands with well-wishers at a suburban Vancouver high school. "The media say Prince William is shy, but he's not at all," Andrew Woodruff, 17, told a newspaper after hosting the young prince at the school. "(He) was really open and social. He asked if I played an instrument and said he used to play drums, trumpet and piano, but not any more."

Later, William eagerly donned a jacket and hat like those worn by Canada's Olympic team, then struck a rap

Young girls reach for the hand of Prince William as he arrives at a school in Burnaby, March 24, 1998. (Frank Gunn)

Prince William jokes with his father Prince Charles after being presented with a jacket and hat from the Canadian Olympic team uniform at a environmental heritage event in Vancouver, March 24, 1998. (Chuck Stoody)

pose for his smiling father, a striking image that was used in papers around the world. William's apparent good mood continued on the slopes of Whistler as he posed with his father and brother in a brief photo opportunity engineered by Buckingham Palace in exchange for privacy during the rest of the vacation.

William, second in line to the throne, was cast in the part of future king when he was born June 21, 1982. He went to public school and now attends the exclusive Eton College. His birth was seen as a confirmation of a fairytale romance. But he was caught in the crossfire when the marriage collapsed. Various accounts depicted William trying to ease his mother's distress during the tumult.

Now comes the challenge of handling fame that has intensified with her death. He's in the spotlight at a time when there is considerable debate about the future of the House of Windsor. "Wills might take comfort in the fact that he is single- handedly persuading a generation of women that the monarchy might be an institution worth saving after all," said the *Evening Standard*.

But William's role in all this remains to be seen. For now, his father appears to favour him having as much freedom as possible.
— *by Ian Bailey*

Prince William (left) and Prince Harry (centre) share a laugh behind their father Prince Charles' back during a guest signing at a school for the deaf in Burnaby, March 24, 1998. (Frank Gunn)

SOPHIE AND EDWARD WIN HEARTS
ON LOW-KEY VISIT

ST. JOHN'S, NEWFOUNDLAND, JULY 18, 2000 (CP) – The first foreign tour by Edward and Sophie, the Earl and Countess of Wessex, was nothing short of a public-relations coup. The subdued, five-day visit to Canada, which ended Tuesday in St. John's, succeeded by highlighting the down-to-earth style of Sophie – who also happens to be a public-relations executive.

The Royal Family's newest member won hearts by easily mingling with the crowds, petting a rodent's nose, eating french fries and asking for a chocolate shake. While attending a rally for youth on a high school soccer field in St. John's, the countess chatted with at least as many awkward teenagers as her husband did despite a light drizzle.

"I figured she would be more snobby, but she was

Edward and Sophie, the Earl and Countess of Wessex, drive in a golf cart in Brudenell, P.E.I., July 15, 2000. (Andrew Vaughan)

real nice," said Victor Rumbolt, 16, of Stephenville, Newfoundland. "She liked chatting and she'd crack a joke every now and then."

But the 35-year-old countess also showed she has the kind of sophisticated grace worthy of a true royal. On Saturday, she attended a dinner in Charlottetown wearing a stunning, champagne-coloured silk gown and the diamond tiara she wore at her wedding to Edward a year ago. Most royal watchers were simply dazzled by Sophie.

"She's going to be another royal star," said Pat McFarlaine, a tourist from Texas who was visiting Prince Edward Island when he saw Sophie in Brudenell. As expected, there were frequent comparisons with the glamorous Diana, Princess of Wales, who was killed in a Paris car crash three years ago. But Sophie's warm charm seemed to extend beyond her good looks. After five days of meeting nervous strangers and making endless small talk, she still laughed easily and often.

Edward and Sophie, the Earl and Countess of Wessex, arrive for a dinner hosted by the government of Canada in Charlottetown, July 15, 2000. (Andrew Vaughan)

The Countess of Wessex adjusts her hat as she accompanies her husband, Prince Edward, on their visit to Charlottetown, July 14, 2000. (Andrew Vaughan)

Earlier, during a walkabout in Charlottetown, she didn't even flinch when she stopped to admire a guinea pig named Max, held by nine-year-old owner Allyson McGuigan. Sophie patted the rodent's nose as a relaxed Edward looked on.

"They are presenting a very happy picture of married bliss," Judy Wade, writer for the London-based celebrity magazine, *OK!*, said in an earlier interview. "That is what the Royal Family desperately needs to rebuild the damage left by three failed marriages."

There's no question that Sophie exudes a kind of confidence that seems rare among new royals. During a tour of a P.E.I. potato-processing plant, she casually munched on french fries and asked for a chocolate shake as Edward cautioned her not to spoil her appetite before a formal dinner.

The couple spent three days touring P.E.I. before travelling Monday to Montreal, where Edward presented Duke of Edinburgh awards to youth from Atlantic Canada. That's when the Queen's youngest son showed he can be a crowd pleaser on his own. After the ceremony, he joked about the tedious and nerve-racking nature of such events.

"Now you can relax," he told the crowd of 300. "It's a bit like banging your head against a brick wall: it's great when it stops."

There were more award presentations Tuesday in Halifax and St. John's. Edward, 36, was expected to be on his own, but many were surprised when Sophie suddenly showed up at both events. Again, the crowds were wowed by the easy manner and sharp style of the former Sophie Rhys-Jones, who was dressed in a bright red blazer and grey skirt.

Yvonne McGrath, who was among a small crowd that gathered outside St. Pius X Church in St. John's, said she was surprised that Sophie seemed so "fresh" on the last day of the royal tour. "I thought she was wonderful," said McGrath. "I was very impressed. She's very pleasant to talk to."

"Beautiful, just spectacular," said Edward Goldberg, an American visiting Halifax. "We don't have this in the States since the Kennedys are gone."

– *by Michael MacDonald*

The Earl and Countess of Wessex, along with Edmonton Mayor Bill Smith and his wife Marlene, walk past an Edmonton Oilers mural in Edmonton, August 5, 2001. (CP)

PRINCE CHARLES PROMISES TO BRING THE KIDS NEXT TIME

SASKATOON, APRIL 28, 2001 (CP) – Prince Charles got the message loud and clear as he left Saskatchewan on Saturday after his first-ever visit to the province.

Come back soon and bring the kids. Or if you can't come, just send the kids.

As much as Saskatchewan residents loved the monarch, their future king, they couldn't suppress their desire to embrace his sons, William and Harry. Even Saskatchewan Premier Lorne Calvert mentioned it when he spoke at a government-sponsored luncheon for the prince who headed to Whitehorse on Saturday evening.

Calvert said the prince had reminded him a few days previous that when King George VI and Queen Elizabeth departed the province after a visit in 1939, the lieutenant governor at the time had invited them to come back soon and bring their kids.

Elder Gordon Oakes presents Prince Charles with a blanket during a naming ceremony at Wanuskewin Heritage Park near Saskatoon, April 28, 2001. (Adrian Wyld)

"Your Royal Highness," Calvert said. "I am implored by my 15-year-old daughter and her friends to say: 'Come again soon, but if it cannot be soon, send the kids.'"

As Calvert's daughter, Stephanie, blushed and the crowd of more than 300 chuckled, Prince Charles said he was listening. "I know only too well that I will have to dispatch my offspring here as soon as I possibly can," he said. "It much amused me the other day to see one particular – I suspect – 15-year-old holding up a sign 'I am your (future) daughter-in-law.'"

Charles' last visit to Canada was a trip to British Columbia with his two sons in 1998. The family made an official stop in Vancouver and spent a private holiday skiing in Whistler. Greeted like pop stars, squealing teenage girls strained to catch a glimpse of Prince William, who was compared to teen heartthrob

Leonardo DiCaprio. This time William is on his gap year between high school and university and is travelling in Africa.

In honour of the prince's visit, the province announced the creation of a $12,000 Prince of Wales Scholarship to assist Grade 11 students in completing high school. The prince said he looked forward to seeing the result of the funding on the futures of young Saskatchewan residents. "I am sure that these scholarships will make a huge difference over the years," he said.

It was another busy day for the 52-year-old prince, who began the morning unveiling a plaque to commemorate the 90th anniversary of the YWCA in Saskatoon, attended a dedication ceremony for a riverbank promenade named in his honour and visited with native elders before flying into Whitehorse.

During his stop at Wanuskewin Heritage Park, a national heritage site northeast of Saskatoon that the Queen visited in 1987, the prince received a Cree name. The prince was wrapped in a white and maroon-patterned

Prince Charles waves as he and Prime Minister Jean Chrétien walk down the red carpet during a welcoming ceremony in Ottawa, Wednesday, April 25, 2001. (Ryan Remiorz)

Prince Charles stops to chat with children who built a snowman for him, complete with a crown, during a visit to Mayo, Yukon, April 29, 2001. (Chuck Stoody)

Charles walks with Junior Canadian Rangers on a portion of the Trans Canada Trail in Mayo, Yukon, April 29, 2001. (Chuck Stoody)

blanket and given the name Kisikawpisim Kamiyowah-pahmikoot, which Cree elders say means "sun watches over him in a good way."

After that, the prince watched a ceremony with traditionally clad native dancers, whirling and dancing in a blur of colours and feathers to the rhythmic beating of a drum. The prince also took a walk with Chief Ben Weenie and spoke about some of the problems facing native people in Canada including health issues such as the high rate of diabetes.

"He talked about non-conventional and conventional approaches," Weenie said after the walk. "Myself, I've been a diabetic for 24 years and I used to sweat a lot and I really believed it helped me and he really agreed with that, the importance of spirituality, the importance of using the things that we have. Some of the medicine people say we come from mother earth so they use plants because they are part of us."

Earlier, after unveiling the YWCA plaque, the personable prince chatted briefly with a young boy who presented him with a picture he had drawn. Justin Katchmar, 9, had waited nearly three hours with his mother and two sisters to present Prince Charles with his drawing of Saskatoon.

"I said, 'Here's a picture for you and your royal family to take home,'" said the beaming blond boy. The prince accepted the drawing graciously after unrolling it to admire the boy's artistic work.

He also stopped to accept a bouquet of flowers from Katherine Grosky, who had parked her wheelchair along a rope that separated the crowd from dignitaries at the plaque unveiling ceremony. Grosky said it was a privilege to chat with the prince.

"Oh, it was just great," she said. "He liked the flowers, I think."

On Friday the prince, an avid gardener and organic farmer, ventured into rural Saskatchewan to visit like-minded producers, but was kept away from farms because of the risk that his entourage might bring the foot-and-mouth disease plaguing Britain to Canada.

– by Craig Wong

Prince Charles is reflected in the roof of his car as he leaves an event in Regina, Friday April 27, 2001.(Adrian Wyld)

OFFICIAL ROYAL TOURS OF CANADA 1951–2002

1951
OCTOBER

Princess Elizabeth and Duke of Edinburgh
Ottawa, Fredericton, Calgary: Elizabeth and
Philip tour Canada the year before Elizabeth
becomes Queen

1954
JULY-AUGUST

Duke of Edinburgh
Ottawa, British Columbia, Northwest
Territories, Quebec: Prince Philip attends
British Empire and Commonwealth Games
in Vancouver

1954
NOVEMBER

Queen Mother
Ottawa: Queen Mother visits Canadian capital

1957
OCTOBER

Queen Elizabeth II and Duke of Edinburgh
Ottawa and Hull: Queen opens first session
of 23rd Parliament

1958
JULY-AUGUST

Princess Margaret
British Columbia, Alberta, Ontario, Quebec,
Nova Scotia: Princess Margaret tours Canada

1959
JULY-AUGUST

Queen Elizabeth II and Duke of Edinburgh
All provinces and territories: Queen opens
the St. Lawrence Seaway

1962
MAY-JUNE

Duke of Edinburgh
Ottawa, Montreal, London, Toronto: Prince
Philip attends Second Commonwealth Study
Conference

1962
JUNE

Queen Mother
Montreal, Ottawa, Toronto, Upper Canada
Village: Queen Mother celebrates the
Centenary of the Black Watch of Canada

1964
OCTOBER

Queen Elizabeth II and Duke of Edinburgh
Charlottetown, Quebec, Ottawa: Queen
commemorates Confederation meetings at
Charlottetown and Quebec in 1864

*(previous pages) Prince Philip, Toronto, October 21, 2001.
(J.P. Moczulski)*

Queen Elizabeth, Ottawa, June 28, 1997. (Kevin Frayer)

1966
MARCH

Duke of Edinburgh
Toronto, Ottawa, Montreal: Prince Philip
presents medals to recipients of The Duke of
Edinburgh's Award

1967
JUNE–JULY

Queen Elizabeth II and Duke of Edinburgh
Ottawa Montreal: Queen attends Centennial
celebrations and Expo 67

1967
JULY

Queen Mother
Nova Scotia, New Brunswick, Prince Edward
Island, Newfoundland: Queen Mother
attends Centennial celebrations

1967
OCTOBER

Princess Margaret and Earl of Snowdon
Toronto, Montreal: Princess Margaret
attends fundraising ball for Princess
Margaret Hospital and visits Expo 67

1967
NOVEMBER

Duke of Edinburgh
Winnipeg and Toronto: Prince Philip opens
Pan American Games and Royal Agricultural
Fair

1969
OCTOBER

Duke of Edinburgh
Ottawa, Newfoundland, New Brunswick,
Quebec, Alberta, British Columbia: Prince
Philip studies operations of The Duke of
Edinburgh Awards scheme

1970
JULY

Prince of Wales
Ottawa: Prince Charles visits Canadian
capital before joining parents on tour

1970
JULY

Queen Elizabeth, Duke of Edinburgh,
Prince Charles and Princess Anne
Manitoba, Northwest Territories: Queen
attends centennial celebrations of Manitoba's
entry into Confederation and the centennial
of the Northwest Territories

1971
MAY

Queen Elizabeth II, Duke of Edinburgh and
Princess Anne
British Columbia: Queen attends Centennial
celebrations of British Columbia's entry into
Confederation

1973
JUNE–JULY

Queen Elizabeth II and Duke of Edinburgh
Ottawa, Ontario, Saskatchewan, Alberta:
Queen hosts Commonwealth Heads of
Government meeting at Rideau Hall; marks
centennials of RCMP and Prince Edward
Island in Confederation

1974
JANUARY

Princess Anne and Captain Mark Phillips
Ottawa, Hull: Princess Anne visits Canada's
capital with her husband

1974 MAY	Princess Margaret and Earl of Snowdon Winnipeg: Princess Margaret attends city of Winnipeg centennial celebrations with her husband	1977 JULY	Duke of York Alberta: Prince Andrew joins Prince Charles to celebrate signing of Treaty 7 and attends Calgary Stampede
1974 JUNE-JULY	Queen Mother Toronto, Montreal: Queen Mother visits Scottish Regiment and presents Queen's Colours to the Black Watch Regiment of Montreal	1977 OCTOBER	Queen Elizabeth II and Duke of Edinburgh Ottawa: Queen celebrates her Silver Jubilee in Canada
1975 APRIL	Prince of Wales Ottawa, Northwest Territories: Prince Charles visits the High Arctic	1978 JULY-AUGUST	Queen Elizabeth II, Duke of Edinburgh, Prince Andrew, Prince Edward Newfoundland, Saskatchewan, Alberta: Queen opens Commonwealth Games in Edmonton
1976 JULY	Queen Elizabeth II, Duke of Edinburgh, Prince of Wales, Prince Andrew and Prince Edward Nova Scotia, New Brunswick, Montreal: Queen and family attend Montreal Summer Olympics, watch Princess Anne and Capt. Mark Phillips participate in equestrian events	1979 APRIL	Prince of Wales British Columbia, Northwest Territories, Manitoba, Ontario: Prince Charles makes a semi-official tour
1977 JULY	Prince of Wales Alberta: Prince Charles celebrates signing of Treaty 7 with Aboriginal Peoples and attends Calgary Stampede	1979 JUNE-JULY	Queen Mother Halifax, Toronto: Queen Mother presents Queen's Colours to Maritime Command and attends 120th running of the Queen's Plate
		1979 NOVEMBER	Princess Anne Ontario: Princess Anne visits Canadian regiments in Kingston, Owen Sound and Ottawa

1980 MARCH-APRIL	**Prince of Wales** Ottawa, British Columbia: Prince visits Pearson College of the Pacific
1980 MAY-JUNE	**Duke of Edinburgh** Ontario, Alberta, Quebec: Prince Philip attends Duke of Edinburgh's Fifth Commonwealth study conference
1980 JULY	**Princess Margaret** Saskatchewan, Alberta: Princess Margaret commemorates 75th anniversary of Saskatchewan and Alberta entering Confederation
1981 JULY	**Queen Mother** Ontario: Queen Mother attends running of the Queen's Plate and bicentennial celebrations for Niagara-on-the-Lake
1981 JULY	**Princess Margaret** Ontario: Princess Margaret tours northern and southwestern Ontario
1982 APRIL	**Queen Elizabeth II and Duke of Edinburgh** Ottawa: Queen signs Constitution Act, 1982
1982 JULY	**Princess Anne** Yukon, Saskatchewan, Manitoba: Princess Anne celebrates bicentennials of Gravelbourg, Estevan, Almeda, Moosomin, Saskatoon
1983 MARCH	**Queen Elizabeth II and Duke of Edinburgh** British Columbia: Queen visits after touring U.S. west coast
1983 JUNE-JULY	**Prince and Princess of Wales** Nova Scotia, New Brunswick, Prince Edward Island, Newfoundland, Alberta: Prince Charles and Diana commemorate the 200th anniversary of the United Empire Loyalists settling in the Atlantic provinces and open the 1983 World University Games in Edmonton
1984 SEPTEMBER	**Queen Elizabeth II and Duke of Edinburgh** New Brunswick, Ontario, Manitoba: Queen celebrates bicentennial of Ontario
1985 JUNE	**Duke of York** New Brunswick, Nova Scotia, Ontario: Prince Andrew attends bicentennial celebrations in Fredericton, Saint John and Sydney, and opens Peterborough liftlock activity centre
1985 JULY	**Queen Mother** Ontario, Alberta: Queen Mother attends running of the Queen's Plate

| 1985 | Duke of Edinburgh |
| AUGUST | Alberta: Prince Philip attends Centennial of Parks Canada and dedicates Lake Louise as a World Heritage Site |

| 1986 | Prince and Princess of Wales |
| APRIL-MAY | British Columbia: Prince Charles and Diana resume their tour of Canada begun in 1983 |

| 1986 | Princess Margaret |
| JULY | Vancouver: Princess Margaret attends Expo 86 |

| 1986 | Princess Anne |
| JUNE | Alberta, Ontario, New Brunswick: Princess Anne visits site of 1988 Winter Olympics as President of the British Olympic Association and inaugurates Equine Research Centre at University of Guelph |

| 1987 | Queen Mother |
| JUNE | Ottawa, Montreal: Queen Mother celebrates 125th anniversary of the Black Watch |

| 1987 | Earl of Wessex |
| JUNE | Nova Scotia, Prince Edward Island: Prince Edward tours Maritime provinces alone |

| 1987 | Duke and Duchess of York |
| JULY-AUGUST | Ontario, Manitoba, Alberta, Yukon: Prince Andrew and Sarah make first tour of Canada |

| 1987 | Queen Elizabeth II and Duke of Edinburgh |
| OCTOBER | British Columbia, Saskatchewan, Quebec: Queen opens legislative session in Victoria and attends heads of government meeting |

| 1988 | Earl Of Wessex |
| JUNE | Ontario, Newfoundland: Prince Edward presents Duke of Edinburgh Award and dedicates Gros Morne National Park as a World Heritage Site |

| 1988 | Princess Margaret |
| JULY | Nova Scotia, Ontario: Princess Margaret commemorates 75th anniversary of Nova Scotia's Women's Institute, attends the running of the Queen's Plate |

| 1989 | Duke of Edinburgh |
| MAY | Quebec: Prince Philip attends meeting of Montreal Canadian Club, 35th anniversary of University of Sherbrooke |

1989 JULY	Queen Mother Ontario: Queen attends Queen's Plate and unveils statue of Sir Frederick Banting in London	1992 JUNE-JULY	Queen Elizabeth II Ottawa, Hull: Queen visits to mark 125th anniversary of Confederation and 40th anniversary of accession
1989 JULY	Duke and Duchess of York Prince Edward Island, Quebec, Saskatchewan, Ottawa: Prince Andrew and Sarah resume their tour of Canada begun in 1987	1994 AUGUST	Queen Elizabeth II and Duke of Edinburgh Nova Scotia, British Columbia, Northwest Territories: Queen opens Commonwealth Games in Victoria
1990 JUNE-JULY	Queen Elizabeth II Alberta, Ottawa: Queen tours Calgary, Red Deer, Ottawa on her own	1996 APRIL	Prince of Wales Ontario, Manitoba, New Brunswick: Prince Charles tours, without Diana
1990 JULY	Earl of Wessex Manitoba: Prince Edward opens Western Canada Summer Games	1997 JUNE-JULY	Queen Elizabeth II and Duke of Edinburgh Newfoundland, Ontario, Manitoba: Queen celebrates re-enactment of arrival of ship the *Matthew* at Bonavista, surveys flood damage in Red River Valley
1991 JUNE-JULY	Princess Anne Newfoundland, Nova Scotia: Princess Anne tours Atlantic provinces	1998 MARCH	Prince of Wales, Prince William, Prince Henry British Columbia: Prince Charles and his sons ski at Whistler
1991 OCTOBER	Prince and Princess of Wales, Prince William, Prince Henry Ontario: Charles and Diana introduce their children to Canadians		

2000 JULY	Earl and Countess of Wessex Prince Edward Island, Newfoundland, Nova Scotia, Quebec: Prince Edward and Sophie tour, present Duke of Edinburch Awards
2001 AUGUST	Earl and Countess of Wessex Edmonton: Prince Edward and Sophie open world track and field championships
2001 JUNE	Prince of Wales Ottawa, Saskatchewan, Yukon: Prince Charles visits Saskatchewan for the first time and hikes Trans-Canada Trail in Yukon
2002 OCTOBER	Queen Elizabeth II and Duke of Edinburgh Nunavut, British Columbia, Manitoba, Ontario, New Brunswick: Queen Elizabeth celebrates her Golden Jubilee in Canada

Note: This list of official tours was compiled from information provided by the Department of Canadian Heritage, www.pch.gc.ca. The Queen and her family have also made many 'private' visits to Canada.

CANADIAN COMMUNITIES VISITED BY THE ROYAL FAMILY, 1951–2002

NEWFOUNDLAND & LABRADOR

St. John's, Gander, Deer Lake, Corner Brook, Stephenville, Carbonear, Harbour Grace, Churchill Falls, Goose Bay, Deer Lake, Strawberry Hill, St. Anthony, L'Anse-aux-Meadows, Red Bay, Bonavista, NorthWest River, Shetshatshiu, Happy Valley, Gander

NOVA SCOTIA

Springhill, Truro, Sydney, Halifax, New Glasgow, Sydney, Louisbourg, Dartmouth, Shelbourne Annapolis Royal, Digby, North Sydney, Pictou, Yarmouth

PRINCE EDWARD ISLAND

Charlottetown, Summerside, Mount Carmel, York, Souris, Basin Head, Fort Amherst

NEW BRUNSWICK

Miramichi City, Caraquet, Charlo, Dalhousie, St-Andrews-by-the Sea, Dartmouth, Fredericton, St John, Moncton, Shediac, Dieppe, Sackville, Riverview Hartland, Grand Falls, St-Léonard, CFB Gagetown, Oromocto

QUEBEC

Hull, Montreal, La Malbaie, Port au Saumon, Port au Persil, Baie Ste Catherine, St. Hyacinthe, Rimouski, Drummondville, Schefferville, Sept-Îles, Gaspé, Port Alfred, Chicoutimi, Arvida, Kénogami, Jonquière, Québec, Trois-Rivières, Beauharmois Lock, St-Lambert Sillery, Cap Tourmente, Rivière-du-Loup, La Pocatière, Lennoxville, Compton

ONTARIO

Owen Sound, Thunder Bay, Niagara Falls, Mississauga, Cobourg, Peterborough, Lakefield, Niagara-on-the-Lake, Ottawa, Brockville, Kingston, Trenton, Toronto, Niagara Falls, Hamilton, St. Catharines, Windsor, North Bay, Kapuskasing, Cornwall, Long Sault, Ingelside, Morrisburg, Iroquois, Brantford, Galt, Guelph, Kitchener, Stratford, London, Chatham, Windsor, Sarnia, Penetanguishene, Midland, Orillia, Washago, Gravenhurst, Torrance, Parry Sound, Sault Ste. Marie, Port Arthur, Fort William, Port Hope, Cambridge, Waterloo, Scarborough, Brampton, Malton, Morrisburg, Prescott, Amherstview, Sudbury, North Bay, Petawawa, Pembroke

MANITOBA

St. Malo, Selkirk, Gillam, Churchill, Brandon, Portage la Prairie, Winnipeg, Thompson, Gillan, Flin Flon, Norway House, Swan River, The Pas, Dauphin, Clear Lake, Brandon, Baily Farm, Oakville, Carman, Beauséjour, Lower Fort Garry, Dauphin, Brandon, Dugald, Red Tail, Thompson

SASKATCHEWAN

Wilcox, Gravelbourg, Estevan, Alameda, Moosomin, Prince Albert, Nipawin, Lac La Ronge, La Ronge, Meadow Lake, Saskatoon, Swift Current, Regina, Uranium City, Unity, Biggar, Dundurn, Hanley, Davidson, Craik, Chamberlain, Moose Jaw, Indian Head, Broadview, Virden Yorkton, Fort Qu'Appelle, Balcarres, Melville, Lloydminster, Yorkton, Canora, Veregin, Kamsack, Kindersley

ALBERTA

Edmonton, Calgary, Banff, Lake Louise, Wainwright, Grande Prairie, Peace River, St. Paul, Vegreville, Fort Saskatchewan, Mundare, Chipman, Lamont, Bruderheim, Fort Edmonton, Medicine Hat, Head-Smash-In Buffalo Jump

BRITISH COLUMBIA

Victoria, Vancouver, Tofino, Kelowna, Vernon, Penticton, William Lake, Comox, Nanaimo, Kamloops, New Westminster, Esquimalt, Twin Island, Prince Rupert, Khutzeymateen Valley, Whistler, Fort St. John, Comox, Courtenay, Langley, Prince George, Quesnel, William Lake, Okanagan, Abbotsford, Royal Roads, Penticton, Chilliwack, Field, Golden, Revelstoke, Sicamous, Ashcroft, Spence's Bridge, Lytton, Boston Bar, Hope, Chemainus, Duncan, Terrace

YUKON

Whitehorse, Dawson City, Mayo, Haynes Junction, Kluane Park

NORTHWEST TERRITORIES

Yellowknife, Rankin Inlet, Iqaluit

Note: This list of communities was compiled from information provided by the Department of Canadian Heritage, www.pch.gc.ca

MAJOR EVENTS IN THE LIFE OF
HER MAJESTY QUEEN ELIZABETH II

APRIL 21, 1926: Elizabeth Alexandra Mary is born at her maternal grandparents' home in London.

DECEMBER 11, 1936: Her father, George VI, accedes to the throne after the abdication of his brother, Edward VIII. Elizabeth is 10.

OCTOBER 13, 1940: During an air raid on London, Elizabeth's voice is broadcast for the first time, in a four-minute address in which the 14-year-old princess says British children are "full of cheerfulness and courage" and bearing their share of the "danger and sadness of war."

APRIL 21, 1944: Elizabeth turns 18, becomes a counsellor of state, and officially starts to fill in for her father when he is out of the country.

JULY 9, 1947: Elizabeth's engagement to Philip Mountbatten is announced, cheering Britons sick of postwar austerity.

NOVEMBER 20, 1947: Elizabeth and Philip marry at Westminster Abbey in a ceremony listened to on radio through-out the world. The day is declared a national holiday; it is the largest public celebration since the victory parade at the end of the war. Canadian Prime Minister Mackenzie King attends, and Canada sends antique silver and a mink coat as a gift.

NOVEMBER 14, 1948: Prince Charles is born at Buckingham Palace. The first news reports in Canada mistakenly announce that a girl has been born.

AUGUST 15, 1950: Elizabeth gives birth to her only daughter, Princess Anne.

OCTOBER 2, 1951: Princess Elizabeth, accompanied by the Duke of Edinburgh, arrives in Quebec City for a six-week visit to Canada, her first. A crowd of 500,000, described as "almost uncontrollable," greet them in Toronto.

FEBRUARY 6, 1952: King George VI dies while Elizabeth is touring Africa.

JUNE 2, 1953: The Queen's coronation, at Westminster Abbey in front of world leaders, is the first coronation of a British monarch transmitted over television.

DECEMBER 25, 1957: The Queen makes her annual Christmas broadcast on television for the first time, shown throughout the Commonwealth.

JUNE 18, 1959: The Queen arrives in Canada for her first major tour as the ruling monarch. She and the Duke of Edinburgh visit all provinces and territories over six weeks. She officially opens the St. Lawrence Seaway.

FEBRUARY 19, 1960: Prince Andrew is born, putting him second in line to the throne.

MARCH 10, 1964: The Queen's last child, Edward, is born.

JANUARY 28, 1965: The Queen signs the act proclaiming the Maple Leaf as Canada's flag.

JUNE 1977: The Queen's Silver Jubilee is celebrated. In the jubilee year the Queen and the Duke of Edinburgh travel some 90,000 kilometres to events throughout the Commonwealth.

JULY 29, 1981: The Queen's eldest son, Charles, marries Diana Spencer at St. Paul's Cathedral.

APRIL 17, 1982: The Queen signs the act proclaiming Canada's Constitution.

JUNE 21, 1982: Diana, Princess of Wales, gives birth to her first child, William Arthur Philip Louis, the Queen's grandson and second in line to the throne.

NOVEMBER 20, 1992: Windsor Castle, one of the Queen's major residences, is seriously damaged by fire.

NOVEMBER 24, 1992: The Queen makes an uncharacteristically frank speech, in which she describes 1992 as an "*annus horribilis*" for her.

DECEMBER 9, 1992: The separation of the Prince and Princess of Wales is announced.

JULY 12, 1996: Charles and Diana agree on the terms of their divorce, ending their 15-year marriage, a watershed moment for the Royal Family.

AUGUST 31, 1997: Diana is killed in a car accident in Paris. The Queen is criticized for not breaking convention and flying the flag above Buckingham Palace at half-mast after Diana's death.

AUGUST 4, 2000: The Queen joins her mother on the balcony of Buckingham Palace as tens of thousands of people wish the Queen Mother well on her 100th birthday.

FEBRUARY 6, 2002: The Queen marks the 50th anniversary of the death of her father, King George VI, and her ascension to the throne quietly, attending a church service and opening a cancer hospital.

FEBRUARY 9, 2002: Princess Margaret dies, at the age of 71, after a stroke and several years of ill health.

MARCH 30, 2002: The Queen Mother dies at the age of 101. Hundreds of thousands of Britons wait in line for hours to view her coffin at Westminster Palace.

JUNE 4, 2002: Official Golden Jubilee celebrations are held in London, which attract a million people to the streets. They include concerts, parades, church service and a ceremonial procession where the Queen rides in the rarely seen Gold State Coach.

OCTOBER 4, 2002: Queen and Duke of Edinburgh arrive in Iqaluit, Nunavut, to begin Golden Jubilee tour of Canada.